FINANCIAL INSTITUTIONS AND SERVICES

BUILDING THE FINANCIAL CAPABILITY OF YOUNG AMERICANS

RECOMMENDATIONS AND RESOURCES

FINANCIAL INSTITUTIONS AND SERVICES

Additional books in this series can be found on Nova's website under the Series tab.

Additional e-books in this series can be found on Nova's website under the e-book tab.

FINANCIAL INSTITUTIONS AND SERVICES

BUILDING THE FINANCIAL CAPABILITY OF YOUNG AMERICANS

RECOMMENDATIONS AND RESOURCES

ANTHONY HODGES
EDITOR

nova publishers
New York

NOTICE TO THE READER

Library of Congress Cataloging-in-Publication Data

ISBN: 978-1-63484-333-1

Published by Nova Science Publishers, Inc. † New York

CONTENTS

PREFACE

Guided by the principle that all young Americans should be equipped with the knowledge and skills necessary to make smart decisions about their finances, this book offers recommendations for government, individual commitments to action, and best practices for improving the financial capability of the nation's youth. The book also addresses frequently asked questions that may arise as financial institutions collaborate with schools, local and state governments, non-profits, or corporate entities to facilitate youth savings and financial education programs.

In: Building the Financial Capability …
Editor: Anthony Hodges
ISBN: 978-1-63484-333-1

Chapter 1

PRESIDENT'S ADVISORY COUNCIL ON FINANCIAL CAPABILITY FOR YOUNG AMERICANS: FINAL REPORT*

CHAIRMAN'S LETTER

The Honorable Barack Obama
President of the United States
The White House
Washington, D.C.

The Honorable Jacob J. Lew
Secretary of the Treasury
Department of the Treasury
Washington, D.C.

Dear Mr. President, Secretary Lew, and fellow citizens:

I have been honored to serve as Chairman of the President's Advisory Council on Financial Capability for Young Americans. During the two years of the Council's charter, we have examined the state of financial capability

---

* This is an edited, reformatted and augmented version of a report issued by the U.S. Treasury Department, June 2015.

among the nation's young people and now submit to you our recommendations for action and dissemination.

We are guided by the principle that all American young people must be equipped with the knowledge and skills necessary to make smart decisions about their finances. Our recommendations address a broad range of important issues:

- Provide and improve access to financial education, services and products, particularly for underserved Americans.
- Use technology to improve scalability and enhance the effectiveness of proven tactics.
- Build and enhance what exists, identify gaps and offer improvements.
- Collect and share knowledge to ensure that no one should have to start from scratch in the field of financial capability.

To tackle these issues, the Council conducted its activities through four working groups. Led by Marc Morial, the Financial Education for Children Working Group developed a plan to pilot a demonstration that tests the hypothesis that if teachers become more comfortable and confident with personal finance topics and better understand effective strategies for teaching these topics, then they will be more competent in teaching them to students.

Carol Quillen led the Post-Secondary Education Working Group, which focused on helping low-income and minority youth to make informed decisions about post-secondary education. They developed a design brief for tools to aid students in making financial decisions around higher education and how to pay for it.

Council Vice-Chair José Cisneros led the Cities and Communities Working Group.

This group focused on the important role that cities and communities play in building financial capability, which extends to building financial education into youth training and employment programs, supporting and promoting Child Savings Accounts policy and programs, and taking action to protect young people from financial abuse.

Across all of the working groups, the Council sought to incorporate innovation and technology to promote financial capability products and tools for young people in order to improve scalability and enhance the effectiveness. Charles Scharf led the Technology Working Group, which worked closely with the other working groups to develop their recommendations, including the teacher training demonstration project, post-secondary decision-making tool, and specific technology-based actions to expand financial access to millions of un- and underbanked young Americans.

Throughout this work, I have personally identified two opportunities of utmost importance. First, it is important that children study financial topics in public schools starting at an early age. Second, we must encourage financial service companies, local businesses, nonprofit providers, foundations and other professionals to foster partnerships with schools to strengthen learning opportunities and provide mentors and role models for children.

In addition to recommendations and ideas into action that support these areas of opportunity, the Council has highlighted cities and states that are making progress toward strengthening financial education in public schools and fostering school partnerships with private sector partners:

- **Chicago**: In March 2015, the Council recognized Chicago as a 'model city' for its commitment to developing a citywide comprehensive financial education strategy. Over three years, the Chicago Financial Education Initiative will bring together city agencies and financial education providers for the first time to develop and enact a plan to make financial education accessible to all youth, parents and community members in Chicago.
- **Baltimore**: In May 2015, the Council highlighted the value of integrating financial concepts throughout the K-12 curriculum, such as those in place in Maryland, to prepare all youth to be financially capable adults and college and career ready.
- **New York City**: In June 2015, the Council highlighted the importance of financial literacy education for K-12 students and noted a partnership between the Council for Economic Education and W!SE to provide financial literacy certification to high school students.

In sum, our young people deserve to have the knowledge, skills, and confidence to successfully handle their personal and household finances as they grow into adulthood. Financial capability empowers us as citizens of a democracy. It allows us to better participate in critical policy debates that will shape our future for decades to come.

Sincerely,

John W. Rogers, Jr., Chair

EXECUTIVE SUMMARY

Executive Order 13646, signed on June 25, 2013, created the President's Advisory Council on Financial Capability for Young Americans to advise the President and the Secretary of the Treasury on how to promote the financial capability of young Americans. Financial capability means having the requisite knowledge, skills and access to manage financial resources prudently and effectively. In order to promote financial capability, we recommend ways to empower individuals to make informed choices; plan and set goals; avoid pitfalls; know where to seek help; and take other actions to better their present and long-term financial well-being. We also take into consideration the particular needs of traditionally underserved populations, recognizing that building financial capability is especially critical to enable upward economic mobility.

Our Council focuses on encouraging financial capability among young people in schools, families, communities and the workplace. By starting early, young people can learn the difference between wants and needs, the power of saving, and the productive role that money can play in their lives. Age-appropriate money skills and habits will make our young people better equipped to tackle more complex financial decisions regarding the financing of higher education and saving for emergencies and retirement. These decisions have lasting consequences for financial security.

This report first summarizes our findings on why building the financial capability of young people is important and the challenges that young people are facing. The report then identifies current progress and promising approaches in the area of building financial capability. Subsequently, the report explains our recommendations and commitments, called *Ideas in Action*, for further progress. These include the following:

- We note ways to better prepare teachers to implement financial education in the classroom using the power of technology.
- We identify the importance of equipping young people with both information and guidance so they can navigate the critical and complex decisions related to postsecondary education and how to pay for it.
- We recognize the uniquely powerful roles that cities and communities can play like connecting young people to appropriate financial products and tools through youth employment programs.

- We appreciate the need to assess how to better protect the identity and credit histories of young people.

Our recommendations are based on evidence of effectiveness; and accordingly, details of our research findings and reasoning are located in the appendices as each subcommittee's working group report.

We hope that the recommendations, ideas in action, and resources identified in this report will spur progress by the President, his Administration, and various levels of government and organizations across sectors toward improving the financial capability of more young Americans.

INTRODUCTION

We are honored to serve in an advisory capacity to President Barack Obama, whose investment in American financial capability is demonstrated by his appointment of two Presidential Advisory Councils on this matter. Each Council builds on previous work, including that of the Council appointed by President George W. Bush in 2008.

The 127 million young Americans under age 30[1] represent America's workforce of today and tomorrow. They help drive our economy and their actions will shape confidence and growth for our country. How they use and understand financial resources, and their abilities to obtain education and jobs, manage debt and daily expenses, overcome setbacks and plan and invest in their futures are a concern for the nation as a whole. The Council hopes the findings and ideas in this report contribute to attaining a more financially capable population.

What We Know About Young Americans' Financial Capability

Young Americans are part of the global economy and workforce. Their financial skills and knowledge will determine how successful our economy will be in the years ahead.

However, there is reason for concern. Fifteen-year-old American students fell short of global financial literacy expectations in 2012 in the first large-scale global financial literacy assessment. The Programme for International Student Assessment (PISA) evaluated students in 18 countries on their ability to apply mathematical skills and basic financial concepts to real world situations. The United States' mean score ranked ninth; Shanghai-China ranked first; and Colombia ranked last. As troubling as these findings may be, the underlying facts demonstrate a concerning picture of the disparities in financial capability by socio-economic status in the United States. According to the PISA study, low-income and minority students were much more likely to score lower than their peers. [2]

Beyond the data presented by the PISA, many data points show that Millennials — young adults — are struggling more than older generations with money management and financial literacy. For example, Millennials have a higher rate of being unbanked than older generations, and they are less likely to pay off their full credit card balance at the end of each month, as well as demonstrating other signs of financial stress.[3] These discrepancies may hinder Millennials' opportunity and ability to attain economic mobility and financial stability.

Our concern with low-income and minority youth is true of young adults as well. Female and minority young adults lag behind their male and white peers; and lower-income millennial households are financially stressed more than their higher-income peers.[4]

Young people of color particularly show evidence of financial challenges. For example, compared to whites, they are more likely to spend more than their income and are more likely to have student loan debt. Lower-income young households find it more difficult to make ends meet, and are less likely to have retirement accounts, mortgages, non-retirement investment accounts or rainy day funds.[5]

While evidence is scarcer on the financial capability of children under age 15, we believe that today's teens and young adults who lack financial capability not long ago were children who did not have opportunities to gain financial knowledge and skills. Despite the clear need for financial education for young people to make sound decisions and have more positive outcomes, too many children do not obtain financial education early in their lives.

Preparing Young Americans for the Future

Given the challenges that young people face, it is clear that financial capability holds great value to individuals, communities, and the nation as a whole. Building financial capability for youth better positions them for the critical crossroads that they will face – whether deciding how much to spend or making an informed decision about post-secondary education – and enables them to improve their financial well-being.

All of these choices can have long-term impacts on financial well-being and opportunities for upward economic mobility. Educating children early, as part of their elementary and secondary education, is critical to prepare them for the paths they will take as adults. In early adulthood, young people generally make financial decisions that have long-term impacts at two critical junctures: choosing post-secondary education and managing their first earnings. All young people should thoughtfully evaluate educational options and income potential. In order to do so, we must provide them with sufficient information to understand the consequences and implications of their choices. It is evident that information and understanding can be enhanced by the opportunity to gain hands-on experience with real financial products and services that meet their needs and allow them to gain experience in money management.

The financial well-being of young Americans can be greatly enhanced by higher learning. Yet, financing higher education, particularly four-year programs, poses its own set of financial questions. As tuition and associated costs have escalated, so has student borrowing.[6] Preparing young people means addressing this issue. Student debt can compromise their ability to handle unexpected expenses caused by job loss, economic shocks and medical events. Although financial capability cannot remove these common challenges, it will equip young Americans to be knowledgeable when they arise.

Fortunately, young Americans live in a technology-rich and highly interactive world that provides ample access to information. Over 80 percent of American teens and upwards of 90 percent of young adults own smartphones.[7] For these young Americans, technology is not merely a tool. It fundamentally shapes the way in which they interact with the world. A young person can order food online, buy movie tickets, hold a text conversation with his or her closest friend, and rent a car all from a mobile device. This resulting generation of digital natives has extremely high expectations around technology and incorporates it into every aspect of their lives.

Perhaps more importantly, technology has significantly impacted the way in which these students learn. In a world where people can access information anytime and anywhere, it is far less important that today's students — the workers of the future — memorize facts and figures. It is absolutely essential that they possess the skills and mindset necessary to seek out, critically analyze, synthesize, and apply the right knowledge at the right time.

Consequently these same attributes are key to consumers' ability to effectively manage their financial lives in an increasingly complex and rapidly changing financial landscape.

In recent years, the broader education community has begun to recognize that today's technology-rich environment has huge implications for how students learn, and has begun to incorporate blended learning strategies to better meet students' needs. The financial capability community must do no less. In order to achieve our goal of a financially capable America, all stakeholders, including educators, content providers, federal, state, tribal and local agencies, and nonprofits must ensure that young people have access to more engaging, technology-enriched blended learning experiences that allow for learning inside and outside of the classroom. In line with the best-in-class examples from the broader education space, these experiences should be highly interactive, intuitive, individualized, and relevant. Above all, we must embrace innovation in financial education to a far greater extent while simultaneously supporting greater evaluation and rigor to ensure that our young people are receiving best-in-class financial education and financial capability training.

The evidence is clear that access to safe and appropriate financial products that meet the needs of young people helps them gain financial capability, especially when young people are earning income through a job. Recent analysis of data from the 2012 National Financial Capability Study indicates that young adults who have both financial education and savings accounts are financially more sound than their peers lacking either or both, even among low-income young adults.[8] Young people should have the opportunity to access their wages safely and the ability to use both transaction and savings products to build sound financial habits. Financial education should be tied to these products to maximize the value of both.

Only by combining this next generation of financial education and training with access to high-quality and appropriate financial products can we ensure that young Americans have the greatest opportunity for financial capability.

Meaningful Progress in the Field

Parents, educators, nonprofits, for-profits, and federal, tribal, state and local agencies constantly innovate and refine approaches to building financial capability. Throughout this report and the appendices, we highlight a number of important available resources and efforts that are underway. Below are a few examples that demonstrate the range of organizations involved in financial capability, the diverse audiences that they serve, and the various channels that they use.

- The Jump$tart Teacher Training Alliance is a coalition of several financial education organizations working together to build a teacher training model with proven results. After the training, which focuses on raising teachers' financial literacy and confidence, 80 percent of participants say they feel more confident teaching personal finance (up from 38 percent), and 90 percent actually integrated financial education into their classroom instruction (up from 61 percent).[9]
- The President's Advisory Council on Financial Capability inspired and encouraged development of more than 110 local financial capability councils across the country. Additionally, the Cities for Financial Empowerment (CFE) Coalition, launched in 2008, and the Cities for Financial Empowerment Fund, launched in April 2012, work with mayors and city leaders to support financial empowerment strategies within municipal services and to establish partnerships between the public and private sectors to integrate financial empowerment services with programs such as workforce development, public housing and domestic violence protection. Among its many accomplishments are the nationally-focused Bank On 2.0 program which provides accessible, safe, and affordable financial products and services and national replication of Financial Empowerment Centers to provide one-on-one counseling and assistance to underserved individuals and families.
- The U.S. Department of Education and the Consumer Financial Protection Bureau have made available numerous consumer-friendly resources to help students and their families and advisors navigate higher education choices and financing. These include *College Scorecard, Financial Aid Shopping Sheet,* www.studentaid.gov, www.studentloans.gov and http://www.consumerfinance.gov/paying-for-college/. The latter, for example, enables students to compare college costs and financial aid offers as well as access information and advice on ways to optimize student loan repayment options. Additionally, the Department of Education has made substantial progress in simplifying the Free Application for Federal Student Aid (FAFSA) in recent years, leading to more students and their

families completing this valuable step to obtaining help in paying for college.

- Private sector innovators — both for-profit and social enterprises — have developed numerous computer- and mobile-based tools to engage young people with learning about and more effectively managing their money. These include components such as games, challenges, interactive lessons, videos, and social media elements.

Actionable Focus Areas

This Council identified several action areas where focused effort can build on previous work to improve financial capability for young people, including several areas where many dedicated professionals and volunteers already work to provide financial education and access. The nation's work in these spheres of influence must continue and use proven and new solutions to overcome barriers.

Primary and Secondary Education

Students begin their formal education in pre-kindergarten and elementary schools, an important setting for their development. A recent study[10] found that young adults who had been exposed to rigorous financial education programs mandated and fully implemented in three states had better credit outcomes later in life relative to young adults from states without financial education mandates or implementation. Further, research indicates that financial education administered to youth as young as elementary school-aged can have a meaningful impact on financial knowledge; and exposure to real-life financial products can increase confidence and interest in managing money.[11]

While schools are a prime venue for learning, schools and educators face ongoing challenges in coping with the amount of critical learning that must fit into existing school days and academic years. Given the pressures of meeting requirements, new standards, and testing, education leaders are looking for solid evidence of effectiveness and efficiency before implementing financial education locally. More schools want to provide financial education yet face a higher bar for inclusion of financial education in their curricula. Demand from educators is driving the need for rigor in course design and assessment. Fortunately, there are research-based resources (see Appendix F) available to help schools seeking to include financial education courses. Using these resources is crucial to effective implementation.

Post-Secondary Education

As a country, we recognize the increasing importance of attaining a post-secondary education and helping students to make informed choices about higher education. Making informed choices includes evaluating and comparing the value of degree programs, understanding financial aid options and determining how to pay for college. In order to be successful at attaining a post-secondary credential, students should understand all aspects of the value of their education as they make these important choices. Students from low-income families or families without experience in attending college are especially challenged in this regard.

Beyond four-year universities, there has been new interest in community colleges and their role in the higher education of nearly 8 million students every year. Trailblazing community colleges, such as in California, have adopted financial capability programs that can be spread to more young adults who will benefit most from higher education and financial capability. Young people who are primarily lower-income represent substantially untapped potential that can be freed through the combination of financial capability and higher education.

Cities and Communities

Many cities and communities combine numerous strategies to impact youth financial capability at the local level, especially for lower-income young people. Local and tribal governments can use the trust of the community and their power to directly reach constituents on a regular basis to effectuate real change. Successful approaches go beyond school-based learning to include accessibility-focused banking programs like Bank On San Francisco,[12] after-school clubs and organizations like Girl Scouts, and key community venues such as public libraries. Because of their scale and ability to collaborate across sectors, localities are especially successful in using holistic strategies that include parents, faith leaders, and others not directly connected to schools.

Technology

Many entrepreneurs across sectors use technologies that resonate with young people to develop innovative approaches to financial education and financial capability. Supporters of such initiatives should insist upon metrics that track changes in behavior and smart synthesis of technology to accomplish learning objectives rather than using technology for technology's sake. Beyond education, technology is increasingly important for accessing the types of financial products and services that help young people manage their money, handle debt, and plan and save for their futures. The speed and convenience brought by mobile devices, for example, into the financial world is likely to enable more products that meet the needs and desires of young people, in ways that can reduce cost and risk. For example, the State of New Jersey, with funding from the Treasury's Financial Empowerment Innovation Fund, is developing and evaluating a program for distributing cash benefits to young adults who are aging out of foster care. The state will distribute the benefits via general purpose reloadable debit cards combined with a mobile app to assist with budgeting and financial decisions. Pilots like this will help the government, financial institutions, and their partners understand how to leverage the benefits of technology to financially empower young people. In another example, the Department of Treasury's new *my*RA product will enable young workers to start an online account to simply, safely, and inexpensively save for their futures. Through www.myra.gov, young Americans can open a portable account that can get them started saving and investing.

Financial Capability Is a Lifelong Priority

Financial capability is a basis for economic prosperity and global competitiveness for our nation as it enables social mobility and financial stability for our citizens. Our challenge is to keep interest high and build on our forward momentum as a country. When we find new and effective ways to promote financial capability, and resources and tools to help achieve it, we need to share those successes. We also need to encourage people to keep building financial capability and, ultimately, achieve financial well-being.

CHARTING THE COURSE

Focus and Objectives

Through its research, consultations, discussions and deliberations the Council helped to determine the best ways to encourage the nation's young people to develop financial knowledge and skills. The Council focused on strategies to promote the use of high-quality financial capability resources and practices in schools, families, communities and elsewhere. It also focused on identifying and developing approaches that are likely to have significant effects on young Americans' financial capability. The Council identified four particularly promising strategies: building strong partnerships between and among governmental (federal state, tribal and local) and private entities; planning and/or developing pilot programs; leveraging technology; and supporting research and evaluation practices.

Approach

The Council conducted its activities through four working groups.

Financial Education for Children, Building the Groundwork of Financial Knowledge Focused on strategies to help children attain high-quality financial education through their schooling, such as through implementation of new curriculum standards, hands-on learning opportunities, and opportunities to learn outside the classroom, particularly to reach low-income students, students of color, English language learners and students with disabilities.

Preparing Young People to Make Decisions about Post-Secondary Education that Prepare Them for Financial Independence

Focused on helping young people, especially low-income and minority youth, to develop the financial knowledge, acquire skills, and leverage available resources so that they can make informed decisions about post-secondary education, as well as the job and economic opportunities that arise following post-secondary education, to lead financially independent lives.

Leveraging Cities and Communities for Financial Capability Leadership

Focused on developing strategies to engage cities, communities, and tribal governments, as models for building the financial capability of youth and young adults, by bringing together community leaders and resources to create places in which more residents, especially low-income, minority, and other underserved residents, are financially empowered.

Encouraging Innovation and Technology to Promote Financial Capability Products and Tools for Young People

Focused on developing frameworks for responsible innovation in support of financial, educational, and other transformational technologies that expand financial access and capability for young Americans, especially in underserved communities; and that help them manage their money, handle debt, and plan, save and invest for the future.

Themes

The full Council reviewed, discussed and approved recommendations and advanced several initiatives reflecting four general themes. Additionally, the Council inspired a number of actions that will build on these recommendations which are described further below.

Providing and improving access to financial education, services and products: Access includes the ability to act upon financial choices for Americans through access to appropriate, safe and affordable financial products and services to help young people get a good financial start.

Leveraging technology: Millennials and younger digital natives still benefit from high-touch intermediaries such as parents, teachers and guidance counselors, as well as seek information and actively learn with digitally-driven tools, games and apps. Newer technologies improve scalability and enhance the effectiveness of proven tactics.

Building on what works: Build and enhance what exists, identify gaps and offer improvements. The best use of limited resources often includes leveraging what already works well. Thoughtfully designed pilot programs with rigorous evaluation help improve work in the field. Also, policymakers need this information to make decisions about implementing initiatives, weigh costs and benefits, and take effective and appropriate action.

Collecting and sharing knowledge: First-time and experienced financial educators alike benefit from recommendations on best practices, vetted resources, innovative breakthroughs and meaningful failures. No one should have to start from scratch in the field of financial capability.

Recommendations and Ideas in Action

Recommendations

The Council's recommendations provide targeted opportunities to improve financial capability, promote lifelong asset building, and empower young Americans to achieve greater financial stability. These recommendations span delivery opportunities such as schools, communities and technologies to positively affect behavioral change from early childhood to emerging adulthood. Many of the Council's recommendations address inspiration, training, technology rewards, economic mobility, and pitfalls for young people throughout their school and college years and continuing into adulthood. Others enhance critical decision points, such as first paychecks and post-secondary education financing. Woven throughout the recommendations is recognition of the importance of harnessing technology and engaging intermediaries in the public and private sector.

Below is a summary of key recommendations of the Council. Information on these and additional recommendations can be found in Appendices A-D: Reports of the Working Groups.

Summary of Recommendations

Aspirational Statement

- All American children must be equipped with the knowledge and skills necessary to make smart decisions about their finances. This is a basic right that must be integrated throughout children's Pre K-12 learning experience to assure that all youth in America have the tools necessary to make sound financial decisions that will allow them to pursue their dreams. Whatever their life's aspirations, whether college bound, career ready or thinking entrepreneurially, this knowledge will enable our young people to compete in a global economy and enhance our nation's economy.

Inform and Simplify Post-Secondary Education Decision Making

- FAFSA (Free Application for Federal Student Aid) should be further simplified, and volunteers and technology should be used to help students complete financial aid forms and receive customized guidance on their post-secondary options.
- Federal student loan repayment options should be more broadly communicated to empower young people to apply and remain enrolled in sustainable repayment plans.
- Governmental agencies should better coordinate to help more students access all available resources to help support them toward completing their post-secondary education.
- Interested students should be able to share their academic information (e.g., test scores and transcripts) with technological

tools that can deliver meaningful and customized information about post-secondary options in a trusted, timely and relevant form.

Engage Communities and Schools

- Youth job training and employment programs should integrate financial education and provide direct deposit to safe and affordable transactional accounts at mainstream financial institutions. Youth job training and employment programs may also connect young people to child savings account programs, individual development accounts and longer-term savings vehicles, including products like *my*RA, to help establish a lifelong habit of saving for their futures.
- Community hubs, such as libraries and community colleges, should be better deployed to connect financial capability resources to individuals and educators.
- Technology should be used to help teachers improve their competence and confidence in teaching students about finance, such as by using online credentials to encourage innovation.
- The United States should participate in the Programme for International Student Assessment's (PISA) 2015 study of the financial knowledge of 15-year-olds.
- Private sector partnerships with state, tribal and local governments should be encouraged in order to facilitate greater adoption of modern, real-time electronic payments solutions and best practices to help young people better manage, move and control their spending.

Improve Identity and Credit Protection and Provide Pathways for Saving

- Identity theft and credit abuse among young people should be examined and combatted through the use of consumer protection tools and private and public sector collaboration.
- Child Savings Accounts and policies should be promoted as a means to increase the likelihood of college attainment.

Addressing Financial Education in School-Based Settings

The Council crafted the following broad aspirational statement to inspire and guide financial educators in their mission to help youth's financial decisions allow them to pursue their dreams and prepare them to compete in a global economy.

> All American children must be equipped with the knowledge and skills necessary to make smart decisions about their finances. This is a basic right that must be integrated throughout children's Pre K-12 learning experience to assure that all youth in America have the tools necessary to make sound financial decisions that will allow them to pursue their dreams. Whatever their life's aspirations, whether college bound, career ready or thinking entrepreneurially this knowledge will enable our young people to compete in a global economy and enhance our nation's economy.

The Council encourages the United States to continue to participate in the Programme for International Student Assessment (PISA) of the financial knowledge of 15-year-olds in the next study in 2015. This valuable assessment helps gauge our global performance in youth financial capability over time and reveals opportunities for improvement.

The United States' poor standings on the PISA study also motivated the Council to spearhead the creation of a teacher training project to help middle school students and teachers nationwide. The Council recommends boosting the competence and confidence of instructors teaching personal finance, while empowering teachers to take control of their own finances. In support of this recommendation, the demonstration pilot will use digital technologies and recognition through micro-credentialing and badging, among other innovations. Research shows overwhelmingly positive response from teachers who have received formal training on personal finance topics through the Jump$tart Teacher Training Alliance, with 99 percent of them thinking that other teachers would find a similar training opportunity helpful.[13] The recommended demonstration pilot will add and test bonus rewards for effectiveness among teachers.

Leveraging Critical Decision Points for Post-Secondary Education

With regard to financing post-secondary education and increasing access to the financial mainstream, the Council recommends support for and promotion of Child Savings Account (CSA) programs and policies across the United States. Research shows that students in families with designated savings for post-secondary education are more likely to enroll in college and graduate, even when the dollar amounts saved are relatively small. Supporting CSA policy can help underserved families who do not have easy and direct access to savings accounts or to programs and incentives that encourage them to save.

The Council also makes a number of policy recommendations to help students and their families with planning, applying for financial aid, and repayment of student loans. The first steps to applying for financial aid — filling out forms — can be a barrier for some students and their families. To prevent people from being intimidated or discouraged by the process, the Council recommends that the federal government simplify the FAFSA (Free Application for Federal Student Aid), making it easier to complete earlier and electronically, including via third-party technology tools, by building on the work of the Administration and Congress. Additionally, the Council recommends offering a mechanism similar to the VITA (Volunteer Income Tax Assistance) program. Trained volunteers would help students and their families with the FAFSA, the CSS (College Scholarship Service) profile, and other state and school-specific forms; and support the development of technology tools that can help students access and file these forms electronically with the appropriate federal, state or tribal government.

The Council also recommends the creation of a simple mechanism for interested students to grant access to selected and relevant academic information (e.g., test scores, transcripts) so that technological tools can deliver meaningful, customized information about postsecondary options in a trusted, timely, and relevant form.

Research shows that 24 percent of millennials think their student loans will be forgiven.[14] The Council also recommends improving and strengthening communications about all available repayment options for federal student loans, including income-driven repayment plans, so that borrowers can seamlessly apply and stay enrolled.

The Council further recommends fostering better coordination between federal and state agencies, including social services organizations, to ensure students are accessing all available resources to help support them as they work toward a post-secondary credential.

The Council identified several key questions that might guide future research, address reasons for drop-outs and defaults, and provide more insight on how and when students and families make decisions about post-secondary education.

Identifying Opportunities for Technology Integration

The Council recommends using the power of technology and one-on-one attention to help students and their families make better decisions about post-secondary education and how to pay for it. In support of this recommendation, the Council developed a blueprint of a design challenge for building a tool that will guide students in making the best financial decisions when selecting a post-secondary institution.

The Council also recommends tailoring financial products and education tools to meet the needs of young people, as well as technology-based actions to expand financial access to millions of un- and underbanked Americans, including the significant percentage of young people among them. These recommendations leverage the opportunity to get young Americans off on the right foot as they begin their financial lives with, for many, their first paychecks from summer jobs. For example, the Council encourages state, tribal, city and community employers to disburse wages electronically via high-quality transaction accounts and promote greater awareness and adoption of electronic payment solutions that meet the needs of young Americans with modern functionalities and tools to help these consumers better manage, move, and control their spending. Localities should partner with responsible financial institutions and other public and private partners to deliver transaction accounts to young people, reducing their dependence on more risky alternative financial services.

Engaging Communities

In its mission to improve upward economic mobility and serve the underserved, the Council particularly recognizes the importance of states, tribes, and local governments in helping the people in their communities. These entities have the trust of the community and the power to directly reach constituents needed to effect real change, especially among low-income, minority, and underserved residents. Successful jurisdictions that share their findings, best practices, and challenges can help other communities. Many have made significant and measurable impact, including, but not limited to the states of Delaware and Wisconsin; the cities of San Francisco, Miami, New York, and Savannah, Ga.; American Indian tribes such as Citizen Potawatomi Nation in Oklahoma and Eastern Band of Cherokee Indians in North Carolina; and several state financial literacy councils in Washington, D.C., Maryland, Tennessee, and Wisconsin.

When young people receive their first paycheck, they are primed to learn more about money management and have a unique opportunity to make a timely and informed choice about their new income. The Council recommends integrating financial capability practices into youth training and employment programs, including financial education, access to direct deposit and safe bank accounts, and regulatory guidance regarding products for young people that enable them to safely learn to manage their money and save.

The President and his Administration can encourage the creation of cross-sector partnerships by calling on business, educational institutions, especially community colleges, other nonprofits, and government to join together to leverage their individual contributions to create comprehensive programs that provide students with a pathway through postsecondary education to jobs and financially secure futures. Programs must be measured and evaluated; and successful programs must be replicated in different regions or grown in scale.

The Council also recommends using existing community hubs, such as libraries and community colleges, to disseminate best practices, tools and resources to local instructors and consumers. For example, there are approximately 119,000 libraries of all types in the United States, including 98,500 public, private and tribal school libraries.[15] Libraries have an important role to play in addressing the growing need and demand for unbiased financial capability content and programs.

Protecting Identities and Credit

Young people need protection in addition to opportunity so that they do not begin adulthood with damaged credit history, whether the cause is unintentional errors or deliberate financial abuse. The Council recommends specific strategies to combat identity theft and credit abuse for young people, particularly vulnerable populations. The Council identifies the need for more research on the scope of the problem, greater public and private sector collaboration, enhanced training for intermediaries, and broader distribution of consumer protection tools and resources for this audience.

Council Ideas in Action

The Council announced several action points by Council members and others that will build upon the findings and recommendations of the Council, and enable the ideas to move into action. These include a post-secondary student mentoring program, a public design challenge, a teacher resource center, and compilations of important examples of best practices, resources and tools in the financial capability field.

Technology Enhancements for Teacher Training Pilot

At the encouragement of, and in coordination with, the Council, PwC, Digital Promise, and the Global Financial Literacy Excellence Center (GFLEC) at the George Washington University are planning a Personal Finance Educator Micro-Credential Project. The project will test the hypothesis that if teachers become more comfortable and confident with personal finance topics, and better understand effective strategies for teaching these topics, they will be more competent in teaching them to students. The project targets teachers who have the greatest opportunity for growth in financial literacy competence — those who do not primarily teach personal finance (focusing on 6th-9th grades). It will provide these teachers with the opportunity to gain recognition for their competence in personal finance instruction through the use of micro-credentials (a form of digital badging). The project also will review the literature and gather insights from teachers and students to uncover research-backed teaching methods, understand the relationship between the micro-credentials and personal finance instruction, and identify gaps in the market for personal finance professional development for teachers. This project will outlive the Council and be managed by Digital Promise with the support of partners, including PwC and other educational organizations.

New Online National Teacher Resource Center

The National Endowment for Financial Education and the Take Charge America Institute at the University of Arizona are building an online national teacher resource center, known as Money Teach (www.moneyteach.org), which will be operational in 2015. The center will provide resources for middle and high school educators of all experience levels; particularly giving new financial education teachers a trusted place to start. Teachers can use shopping cart-type technology to build course plans, drawing on multiple content providers to meet the needs of their learners by class makeup and by the amount of time available to teach the subject. Access to the center will be free. Once built, Money Teach will be able to add highly-regarded content providers, best practices, and input from master teachers. Check NEFE's High School Financial Planning Program site (www.hsfpp.org) and the TCAI site (www.tcainstitute.org/) for updates.

Chicago Financial Education Initiative and Other Local Initiatives

The Council highlights cities, communities, and states that are making progress toward strengthening financial capability through expanding financial education in public schools and fostering school partnerships with private sector partners. As a leading example, over three years, the Chicago Financial Education Initiative will bring together city agencies and financial education providers for the first time to develop and enact a plan to make financial education accessible to all youth, parents and community members. In New York, the Council highlights a partnership between the Council for Economic Education and W!SE to provide financial education and certification to high school students. Additionally, Operation Hope has partnered with a number of financial institutions to open Hope Inside Centers in underserved communities, including Detroit and St. Louis.

Economics Center Math/Financial Literacy Lessons

Building from the Money As You Learn initiative inspired by the prior Advisory Council (www.moneyasyoulearn.org), the Economics Center at the University of Cincinnati has launched a new series of lessons for students in grades 3-8 that integrate math and financial literacy. The new "Math That Makes ¢ents" series was developed in collaboration with the Math Forum at Drexel University, funded by Jump$tart, and supported by the National Endowment for Financial Education.

Summer Jobs and Financial Education for Underserved Youth

The Citi Foundation and Cities for Financial Empowerment Fund expanded its *Summer Jobs Connect* program into the District of Columbia and St. Louis in 2015, joining Chicago, Los Angeles, New York City and San Francisco in providing more than 2,000 low-income youth with summer work experience and access to financial education and appropriate financial services. Summer jobs often are the first experience youth have with formal employment, and serve as a natural opportunity to provide personal financial education. The mayors of each participating city are critical partners in these efforts. Through the Council, Visa partnered with CFE Fund and Citi Foundation to expand access of *Summer Jobs Connect* participants to high quality transaction accounts.

Fellowship to Help Integrate Financial Capability and Youth Employment

Casey Family Programs has committed to sponsoring an Operation HOPE Fellow to help carry out the recommendations of this report, with a particular emphasis on building financial capability through employment. For a year, the Fellow will work with the Department of the Treasury to foster partnerships and expand opportunities for youth to build financial capability through jobs and training programs that offer financial education and access to financial products and services.

Pilot Enhancements to an Existing College Decision-Making Partnership

The Council applauds mentoring partnership programs, such as the one led by e Davidson College, Franklin & Marshall College and the College Advising Corps to train current college students to help underserved students and families to fill out college applications and financial aid forms.

Develop a Design Brief for a Post-Secondary Decision-Making Tool

The Council encourages innovation and collaboration to develop a tool that truly meets students where they are and aids in the actual post-secondary education decision. Moneythink and the Council developed a design brief (See Appendix B) to issue as part of a public challenge wherein individuals and organizations can engage in collaborative online dialogue, regional meet-ups, and further action to build technological solutions for future college students. Moneythink and Visa have begun discussions with a global design company to further develop the design challenge.

Increased Awareness of Student Loan Repayment Programs

Over the past two years, Intuit has raised awareness of the Department of Education's student loan repayment program among its TurboTax and Mint customers. By providing individuals with a prompt to think about repaying their student loans, Intuit has helped to draw thousands of individuals to the federal student loan repayment website. While this is just one example, continuing to draw awareness to the student loan repayment programs will empower people to take control of their financial lives during their transitions from education to the working world.

Expand the Financial Planning Profession and Encourage Volunteerism Among Financial Professionals

An increasingly diverse population of young Americans points to a growing need for an equally diverse workforce of financial planners who can meet the increasing need for competent, fiduciary-level financial advice. Currently, there is a significant under-representation of racial, gender and age diversity within the financial services industry, a segment that continues to experience growth and provide for career opportunities. The Certified

Financial Planner (CFP) Board has established the CFP Board Center for Financial Planning, a broad industry initiative to bring financial services firms, educators, and practitioners together to address the existing talent shortage and workforce development challenges in the financial planning profession. The Center will use a "research to action" approach to build the capacity for the financial planning profession by creating a sustainable supply of new and more diverse advisors to replace the retiring workforce.

Through the new Hamilton Campaign, young adults in the financial profession are being encouraged to provide volunteer financial coaching, drawing on the pro-bono model of the legal profession. This model may encourage more young people to enter into careers in the financial sector.

Treasury Financial Empowerment Innovation Fund

Treasury awarded $6.2 million in contracts to 11 research projects in a competitive process in 2014 from the Financial Empowerment Innovation Fund.[16] These projects will develop, test, and evaluate new ways to empower Americans with their finances and help them access safe and affordable financial products and services. These research projects focus on several areas, including promoting more informed decision making in higher education; promoting innovations in payments and savings; and bringing dynamic financial education to more classrooms. The Fund supports research and analysis by some of the nation's leading innovators and research institutions. The research will develop knowledge and insights, and identify new and effective practices in these areas.

myRA to Help Young People Get Started Saving

Treasury created *my*RA - a simple, safe, and affordable starter savings product which can help young people get started saving for retirement early, and reap the benefits of saving over time. *my*RA is a particularly helpful savings program for young people who face barriers to saving for retirement, such as those who do not have access to a retirement plan through their employers. Young Americans can open a *my*RA account with a minimal amount of savings, and there are no fees to open or maintain *my*RA. Young people can open their account and manage it online, and fund it through payroll deduction, so they can make regular contributions and build a habit of savings for the future.

Recommended Lists for Educators, Policymakers, and Others Interested in Financial Capability

The Council compiled a number of resource lists that guided their recommendations and can be helpful in policy or program development, delivery, and evaluation. These lists help disseminate the collective experience and knowledge of the financial capability community.

I. Best practices for effective financial capability programs — Appendix E.
II. Proven and promising financial capability programs, tools and resources — Appendix F.
III. Effective financial capability assessment guidelines — Appendix E.
IV. Federal financial capability programs — Appendix G, pages.

ACKNOWLEDGMENTS

The Council wishes to thank these individuals for sharing their expertise, insights and opinions, and for their support of the Council's efforts. This list includes individuals who have worked most closely with the Council, but does not include all of the individuals who provided helpful ideas and assistance to the Council.

First	Last	Title	Organization
Christina	Baggao	Development Coordinator	Pacific Asian Consortium in Employment
Meina	Banh	Policy Advisory, Office of Financial Education	Consumer Financial Protection Bureau
Marisa	Bardach	Web and PR Manager	The Beth Kobliner Company
Rebecca	Bird	Associate, Marketing and Communications	National Endowment for Financial Education
Desmond	Brown	Program Specialist, Office of Financial Empowerment	Consumer Financial Protection Bureau
Rosemary	Byrnes	Senior Program Officer, Youth Economic Opportunities	Citi Foundation
Tony	Chang		Visa Inc.
Joel	Chastain	Wilma Mankiller Fellow	National Congress of American Indians

(Continued)

First	Last	Title	Organization
Ellen-Blair	Chube		Ariel Investments
Dr. Lennette	Coleman		Ariel Community Academy
Tyrone	Cosey	Market President, HOPE Center Oakland	Operation HOPE, Inc.
Sarah	Costanza		Guardian Life Insurance Company of America
Sarah	Courteau	Executive Editor	The Beth Kobliner Company
Randolph	Deshields Jr.	Graduate	Guardian Life Insurance Money Management for Life Program
Max	Dickstein	Project Manager	The Beth Kobliner Company
Meredith Beaton	Didier	Special Assistant to the President	Davidson College
Daniel	Dodd-Ramirez	Assistant Director, Office of Financial Empowerment	Consumer Financial Protection Bureau
Teresa	Dyer	Public Policy and Advocacy	Girl Scouts of the USA
Mary Hagerty	Ehrsam	CEO, New York and Division President	Operation HOPE, Inc.
Kristen	Faiferlick	Communications Partnerships Resources Manager	Moneythink
Brian	Fitzgerald		Business Higher Education Forum
Todd	Fox	Vice President	Visa Inc.
Cecilia	Frew		Visa Inc.
Mario	Gage		Ariel Investments
Amias	Gerety	Acting Assistant Secretary for Financial Institutions,	U.S. Department of the Treasury
Dr. Lynne M.	Gilli	Program Manager, Career and Technology Education Instructional Branch	Maryland State Department of Education

First	Last	Title	Organization
Dr. Billy	Hensley	Director of Education	National Endowment for Financial Education
Alice	Hockenbury	Vice President, Public Policy and Advocacy	Girl Scouts of the USA
Christine	Kieffer	Senior Director	FINRA Investor Education Foundation
Jeanie	Kirkiles		The Colony Group
Melissa	Koide	Deputy Assistant Secretary for Consumer Policy Executive Director of the Council	U.S. Department of the Treasury
Kyle	Lierman	Associate Director, Office of Public Engagement	The White House
William	Luecht	Manager, External Affairs CDFI Fund	U.S. Department of the Treasury
Cassandra	McConnell-Tatum	Deputy Assistant Director, Office of Financial Education	Consumer Financial Protection Bureau
Brandee	McHale	President	Citi Foundation, and Director of Corporate Citizenship for Citi
Tracy	Moore, II	Co-Founder	MindBlown Labs
Connie	Moran		Ariel Community Academy
Shaba	Nassar	Policy Advisor Office of Consumer Policy	U.S. Department of the Treasury
Brent	Neiser	Senior Director	National Endowment for Financial Education
Melissa	Netram	Senior Public Policy Manager	Intuit
Lucas Turner	Owens	Public Policy Analyst	Operation HOPE, Inc.
John	Oxtoby		Ariel Investments
Leigh	Phillips	Director	San Francisco Office of Financial Empowerment
Tina	Pizzimenti	Senior Director of Presidential Operations	National Urban League
Valerie	Popp	Editorial Assistant	The Beth Kobliner Company

(Continued)

First	Last	Title	Organization
Louisa	Quittman	Director, Financial Education Designated Federal Official	U.S. Department of the Treasury
Janneke	Ratcliffe	Assistant Director, Office of Financial Education	Consumer Financial Protection Bureau
Lauren	Reid	Advisor, Office of Consumer Policy	U.S. Department of the Treasury
Jonathan	Renfrew		Guardian Life Insurance Company of America
Tracy	Rich		Guardian Life Insurance Company of America
Jena	Roscoe	1st SVP, Chief of Government Relations, Public Policy	Operation HOPE, Inc.
Adrian	Russell	Assistant, Office of Consumer Policy	U.S. Department of the Treasury
Traci	Russ-Wilson	Executive Assistant to the President	Davidson College
Barry	Saik	Senior Vice President and General Manager, Consumer Ecosystem Group	Intuit
Sara	Schapiro		Digital Promise
Leslie	Schnur	Editorial Director	The Beth Kobliner Company
Patricia	Seaman	Senior Director	National Endowment for Financial
			Education
Susan	Sharkey	Director, High School Financial Planning Program	National Endowment for Financial Education
Jennifer	Shoop	Chief Innovation Officer	Moneythink
Nat	Sillin		Visa Inc.
Namoch	Sokhom	Director of Business Development Center	Pacific Asian Consortium in Employment
Bob	Solomon		Ariel Investments
David	Soo	Senior Policy Advisor	U.S. Department of Education

First	Last	Title	Organization
Theresa	Tentes	Executive Administrative Assistant to the President	Skyline College
Lance	Triggs	CEO, Los Angeles and Division President	Operation HOPE, Inc.
Gerri	Walsh	President	FINRA Investor Education Foundation
William	Watson, Ph.D.	Director, SparkPoint Center	Skyline College
John	White	Chief of Staff	Maryland State Department of Education
Valerie	Williams	Graduate	Guardian Life Insurance Money Management for Life Program
Kyle	Williams	Legislative Director of Financial and Housing Policy	National Urban League, Washington Bureau
Jai	Winston		Ariel Investments
Trevin	York	Lead Designer	MindBlown Labs

We also would like to thank President Obama for the opportunity to serve on this Council, and his staff at the White House for all of their assistance and support.

Appendix A: Report of the "Financial Education for Children, Building the Groundwork for Financial Knowledge (Pre K-12)" Working Group

The Pre K-12 Working Group focused on creating a framework — a road map — to guide teachers, districts, communities and organizations (educators) interested in implementing and providing effective financial education to Pre K-12 students in and out of schools nationwide.

The Pre K-12 Working Group recommends the following to increase the financial capability of our nation's youth:

Recommended Broad Aspirational Statement to Guide Financial Capability Efforts for Young Americans

All American children must be equipped with the knowledge and skills necessary to make smart decisions about their finances. This is a basic right that must be integrated throughout children's Pre K-12 learning experience to assure that all youth in America have the tools necessary to make sound financial decisions that will allow them to pursue their dreams. Whatever their life's aspirations, whether college bound, career ready or thinking entrepreneurially, this knowledge will enable our young people to compete in a global economy and enhance our nation's economy.

Recommended Teacher Training Demonstration Project

At the encouragement of and in coordination with the Financial Education for Children and Innovation and Technology working groups of the Council, PwC, Digital Promise and the Global Financial Literacy Excellence Center (GFLEC) at the George Washington University are planning a Personal Finance Educator Micro-Credential Project. The project tests the hypothesis that if teachers become more comfortable and confident with personal finance topics and better understand effective strategies for teaching these topics, they will be more competent in teaching them to students. The project targets teachers who have the greatest opportunity for growth in financial literacy competence — those who do not primarily teach personal finance (focusing on 6th-9th grades). It will provide these teachers with the opportunity to gain recognition for their competence in personal finance instruction through the use of micro-credentials (a form of digital badging). The project also will review the literature and gather insights from teachers and students to uncover research-backed teaching methods, understand the relationship between the micro-credentials and personal finance instruction, and identify gaps in the market for personal finance professional development for teachers. This project will outlive the Council; it will be managed by Digital Promise with the support of partners including PwC and other educational organizations.

Recommended Continued Participation in the Programme for International Student Assessment

The United States' continued participation in the Programme for International Student Assessment (PISA) provides the U.S. with rigorous data that will help identify effective strategies for ensuring that more young Americans – especially disadvantaged young people — develop the mathematical, reasoning and financial skills they will need to successfully navigate the world of money in a rapidly evolving global economy. Data from 2015 and future assessments will allow us to assess our progress since 2012.

The working group also recognizes that many who wish to improve the financial capability of young people face hundreds of choices for curricula, educational materials and evaluation tools. To help them better identify what will best work in their instructional framework, the working group compiled the following lists. [Note: To avoid duplication with the appendices, the lists are not provided here.]

I. Recommended List of Best Practices for Effective Financial Capability Programs — see Appendix E.
II. Recommended List of Proven and Promising Financial Capability Programs, Tools and Resources — see Appendix F.
III. Recommended List of Effective Financial Capability Assessment Guidelines — see Appendix E.
IV. Recommended List of Federal Financial Capability Programs — see Appendix G.

Summary of Background Information Gathering

The working group launched a social media campaign to gather input from the public to inform its final recommendations. The feedback loop used the members' personal and organizations' social media platforms, and the unique hashtags, #FinCap and #PACFCYA, and the trending hashtags, #financial and #math, to gather the feedback. The responses were directed to a dedicated Department of Treasury email account, pacfcya@treasury.gov, and shared with working group members.

Additionally, the Pre K-12 working group convened educators, school policymakers and other key influencers in Maryland, a leader in implementing financial education statewide. The meeting, held in Baltimore, discussed the particular issues facing young people of color in distressed neighborhoods. Participating teachers said they were interested in learning more about resources and partners; that training on how to integrate financial education in the classroom was helpful; and that they were concerned about their shortcomings, e.g., in the math aspects of financial education. Participating students said that financial education was important to them; they need and desire to share it with their families; and 7th and 8th grades were a good time to start.

The working group also held a listening session during Jump$tart's April 2015 stakeholder meeting. Hearing what works and what is needed on the ground helps inform policymakers and stakeholders who can more broadly share the lessons learned. Participants said linking financial education to job readiness has good potential; working closely with mayors is a very productive strategy; and that it would be helpful to have more state and local data on student performance, as well as a template on how to communicate the importance of financial education to state and local governments. Additional discussion recommended that FLEC also focus on non-mainland locations such as Puerto Rico in its financial capability efforts.

The working group received briefings from representatives of federal agencies focused on financial capability and financial well-being of children and youth, including the Department of Education, Consumer Financial Protection Bureau, Federal Deposit Insurance Corporation and the National Credit Union Administration.

The Pre K-12 working group will share and socialize its recommendations with key stakeholders, including teachers, local and state education officials, policymakers, nonprofits and community organizations, and distribute this report widely through various channels and outlets over a six-to-12 month period.

Appendix B: Report of the "Preparing Young People to Make Decisions about Post-Secondary Education That Prepare Them for Financial Independence" Working Group

The Post-Secondary Education Working Group was charged with developing strategies to support better pathways for more students to access post-secondary education, build savings, manage debt and ultimately achieve financial independence and autonomy.

Research shows that attaining a post-secondary degree is an important road to greater lifetime income and economic stability. While the return on investment for post-secondary education is generally strong, many, particularly low- and moderate-income students, are not obtaining those returns. Helping students find programs and degrees that put them on track to meet their goals will result in increased value of the investment in education or training. The benefit of these better choices accrues to students, their families and communities, the institutions they attend, and ultimately, to our whole economy.

In light of these factors, the working group was guided by an overarching theme:

Education is an asset that each person can build from birth; building this asset is crucial for individual autonomy, an educated citizenry and a prosperous, democratic society.

The working group explored existing programs, research findings, anecdotal evidence and best practices in the following four areas:

- Return on investment (ROI) — monetary and societal — of post-secondary education;
- Technological tools that maximize financial decision making and educational mentoring;
- Successful partnerships and connections between sectors (e.g., business, higher education, government, technology) that enable students to thrive; and
- Metrics and measures of success of existing programs and initiatives.

Policy Recommendations

- Build on work done by the Administration and Congress to simplify the FAFSA (Free Application for Federal Student Aid), making it easier to complete.
- Offer a mechanism similar to the VITA (Volunteer Income Tax Assistance) program to aid families in completing financial aid forms, including the FAFSA, the CSS (College Scholarship Service) profile and other state- and school-specific forms, and support the

development of technology and tools that can help students and families access and file these forms.

- Create a simple mechanism for interested students to grant access to selected and relevant academic information (e.g., test scores, transcripts) so that technological tools can deliver meaningful, customized information about post-secondary options in a trusted, timely and relevant form.
- Foster better coordination between federal and state agencies, including social services organizations, to ensure students are accessing all available resources to help support them as they work toward a post-secondary credential.
- Improve and strengthen communications about all available repayment options for federal student loans, including income-driven repayment plans, so that borrowers can easily — and seamlessly apply — and stay enrolled.

Key Findings

- Students and families need information earlier about financing needs, industries and job training, and opportunities after their post-secondary education in order to better understand and make long-term plans. Many students choose paths of study based on their general interests, without a plan for how to get a job with their degree or knowledge of if and where jobs based on their studies are available.
- College, career and financing are not "one size fits all." Many of the students with the most need are non-traditional (for example, many years out of high school, going back to school to finish a degree). There are many job training options that should be considered beyond traditional four-year college, including community college, career technical education certificate programs, career ladder/stackable certificate programs and apprenticeship programs. For underserved students, financing and support is needed not just for tuition, but also to defray other costs, including books, rent, day care, transportation and other "life" costs not directly associated with school. In the case of internships, pay is important for underserved students and, for many, is the deciding factor if they pursue a job program.
- Businesses can provide crucial input to colleges on their workforce needs and the skills students will need for them this should be used to

drive curricula for degree/certificate programs. They also can provide opportunities like internships and apprenticeships.

- A core curriculum, and pathway to creating a personal financial plan, should include learning about spending, saving and consumer protection; consumer credit and debt management; employment, income/compensation and taxes; investing and estate planning; risk management and insurance; and financial decision making and strategic planning.
- Cross-sector partnerships that link financial literacy, education, social/support services and career opportunities, including summer employment and internships, are effective in building financial capability.
- Information about post-secondary options and financial aid will change behavior only if it is trusted, timely and immediately relevant. Help filling out the financial aid forms, in particular, has been shown to increase aid dollars and college attendance.
- Near-peer mentoring and coaching can dramatically impact student persistence, whether in an educational program or a behavior (like good financial management).
- Context matters. For many students, support and social services are as important as financial aid.
- We must engage young people early. Making students aware of the opportunity of post-secondary education earlier (9th grade and earlier when feasible as opposed to 11th) and stressing the importance of the investment makes for better choices and less debt.

Key Questions that Might Guide Future Research

- Why do students drop out?
- Who defaults on student loans and why?
    - What does repayment look like?
    - How do different repayment plans affect the finances of individuals and households?
- How and when are students and families making decisions about college and how to pay for it?
- How can people comprehensively evaluate the choice of school/educational programs in light of the financial capability, present and future, of their families?

- What factors influence success as students transition from college to the labor market?
- When students and families are trying to figure out the cost of college, how should they calculate ROI? Pay? Opportunity?
- How can we create a corps of volunteers to help families fill out the FAFSA as well as the CSS Profile?
- How can we encourage more schools to participate in programs like College Advising Corps and uAspire, which help students and families navigate the higher education process (applying, paying for and graduating) through mentoring and counseling?
- How can the federal student aid program be simplified to close the access gap, minimize the role of the for-profit debt relief industry and minimize the high-stakes consequences of not succeeding the first time around?
- How can technology play a key role in transitioning students from the classroom to the real world?

Calls to Action

Public Challenge for Solutions via Design Brief

We see an opportunity for visionary and technically skilled citizens and organizations to build websites and mobile applications that help young adults make financially healthy, informed decisions about post-secondary schooling and financing. Currently there are a variety of websites and mobile applications on the market that help guide students, parents or counselors with information about schools, their prices, scholarships and financial aid, but none are designed in a way that truly meets students where they are and aids in the actual decision.

To spur innovation and collaboration around this topic, we've composed a design brief, which offers the provocation: "How might we build a tool that guides students in making the best financial decisions when selecting a post-secondary institution?" This design brief will be made available and issued as a challenge to the public, wherein individuals and organizations can engage in collaborative online dialogue, regional meet-ups and further action to organize around this question and begin to build technological solutions for the next generation.

College Access, Decision Making and Matching Programs and Tools

Many colleges and universities have forged relationships with nonprofits that help talented, underserved students apply and enroll in match schools. Such programs include the Posse Foundation, Questbridge, the College Advising Corps, Bottom Line and uAspire. We strongly encourage expanding these partnerships to reach more students.

Davidson College and Franklin & Marshall College (Lancaster, Pa.) are privileged to have a strong partnership with the College Advising Corps (CAC) whereby recent Davidson and F&M graduates mentor high school students from rural communities across North Carolina and Pennsylvania. CAC in partnership with UAspire will work with Davidson and F&M to implement a pilot that trains current college students (at Davidson, F&M, and elsewhere in North Carolina and Pennsylvania) to bolster the impact and reach of the CAC advisors.

As a result of this effort, we will:

- Assist college-bound high school juniors and seniors to help high school students and families in underserved areas fill out financial aid forms in addition to college applications
- Facilitate the opportunity for successful access to and completion of post-secondary education for underserved students

Creation of Cross-Sector Partnerships

The President and his Administration can encourage the creation of cross-sector partnerships by calling on business, educators, nonprofits and government to join together to leverage their individual contributions to create comprehensive programs that provide students with a pathway through post-secondary education to jobs and financially secure futures. Programs must be measured and evaluated, and successful programs replicated in different regions or grown in scale.

Business as a Development Partner

Businesses are underutilized partners in ensuring student success. Businesses and postsecondary institutions can partner to create job pathway programs for students. They can provide: funding; manpower through volunteers; input to educators on jobs available and skills needed; professional development for teachers; and experiential learning and mentoring to students through internships to teach technical skills, office etiquette and resiliency skills.

Goals and Responsibilities

- All partners must agree on the ultimate goals of the program with input from students, educators and businesses.
- Partners must agree on responsibilities for all involved, and there should be an understanding that each partner's level of contribution, responsibility and outcomes from the partnership may vary.
- Senior level buy-in to the goals of the partnership programs from the businesses, nonprofits and educators is crucial to success. The leaders not only must support the funding of the programs, but must set the "tone at the top" to underscore the importance of the program by integrating it into the mission and language of their organization at all levels.

Measures of Success

- Measures of success for short-term and long-term outcomes must be defined at the onset of a partnership program and are crucial to developing a program that can be scaled and replicated.
- Metrics may include measuring knowledge, behavior and ultimately student success in attaining and keeping a job.
- Completion of any post-secondary program in which a student is enrolled, including on-the-job training, apprenticeships, certificate programs and degree programs, is a key predictor of success.

Community Colleges Are a Priority Partner

It is a priority to leverage partnership opportunities with community colleges because they collectively serve approximately 8 million students. Community colleges are excellent conveners for job partnership programs. They can bring together many employers who each can provide a small number of internships to create a larger program, and then vet and provide the pipeline of students to be included.

Community colleges also should leverage local volunteers as mentors to both employers and students. For example, Tennessee Promise announced two free years at community colleges in the state; nearly 90 percent of high school students applied, and more than 9,000 adults volunteered to serve as mentors. Because they are so new, very few current financial capability programs have pointed to best practices and how to pay for post-secondary education. The field does not yet have a common set of metrics or demonstrated success.

We need to document and share promising practices that connect the student to workforce/autonomy by linking academics, mentoring, internship/job placement, financial literacy and paying for debt. These practices should suggest solutions for lack of funding, and demonstrate scalability. Longer term (2-4 years) observation is preferable. Universal access to community colleges is a key factor that will increase the number of students who are able to achieve higher education as an asset.

Providing national support for community colleges to host financial capability support centers would increase accessibility of financial capability support, leverage existing state and federal investments, and create systems change in providing student services to support college completion.

Careers in Financial Planning Present a Strong Option

An increasingly diverse population of young Americans points to a growing need for an equally diverse workforce of financial planners who can meet the increasing need for competent, fiduciary-level financial advice. Currently there is a significant under-representation of racial, gender and age diversity within the financial services industry, a segment that continues to experience growth and provide for career opportunities.

The Certified Financial Planner (CFP) Board has established the CFP Board Center for Financial Planning, a broad industry initiative to bring financial services firms, educators and practitioners together to address the existing talent shortage and workforce development challenges in the financial planning profession. The Center will use a "research to action" approach to build the capacity for the financial planning profession by creating a sustainable supply of new and more diverse advisors to replace the retiring workforce.

Regional Focus Is Crucial for a Successful Partnership

- Jobs: In regions with very large employers or an industry presence (e.g., Hartford, Conn., as the "insurance capital"), these companies can easily partner on programs and help schools to develop curricula for their job needs.
- Students: Many underserved students cannot commute one or more hours for work or school and therefore make their choices based on commuting limitations.

Holistic Approach is Necessary

Beyond technical skills training, job training programs must help students by providing training in:

- Personal presentation and interview skills, and resume writing;
- Communication in the workplace, handling conflict, attitude;
- Resiliency (punctuality, having a backup plan);
- Access to social services; and
- One-on-one mentoring.

In addition, tone is important — these services and trainings must be provided in a dignified manner to the students.

Summary of Background Information Gathering

In order to determine the correct set of recommendations to bring to the Council, the Post-Secondary Education Working Group worked in smaller subsets of the committee to gather information that would inform our discussions/recommendations in the areas of technology, partnerships and mentoring.

In addition to the subgroups, the committee engaged in the following activities:

- In June 2014, members of the working group convened for a daylong meeting at Davidson College (Davidson, N.C.) with the overarching goal of preparing young Americans to make decisions about post-secondary education that will ultimately help them establish financial independence.
    - In addition, during an on-campus lunch, Charlotte-area community members joined the working group for a presentation about the new "Financial Aid Toolkit" developed by the Federal Student Aid (FSA) office at the Department of Education. The toolkit provides online access to a database of financial aid resources for school personnel, community organizations and others who work with students and their families.
- On Monday, March 2, 2015, members of the Post-Secondary Education Working Group met in Washington, D.C., with approximately 30 business, education, government, technology and philanthropic leaders from across the country to discuss creating better pathways for more students to access a post-secondary education, build savings, manage debt, and ultimately achieve financial independence and autonomy.

Design Brief

How might we build a tool that guides students in making the best financial decisions when selecting a post-secondary institution?

Overall Objective

To design a digital tool that aids students in making financial decisions around access to higher education at the point of decision making.

More specifically, there are three tiers of related, time-sensitive decisions that students need support making:

- Identifying affordable college options that meet and reflect an appropriate financial, social and academic fit;
- Getting the best aid package possible;
- Evaluating aid offers based on ROI of the school (and what the student wants to study there), as well as the debt/financial package that a student will receive.

Target Audience

This tool is specifically designed for:

- High school students who are
- Under 18 years of age,
- Have access to reliable Wi-Fi, and
- Have a desire to attend college

Scope of Project

This solution must be digital and should automate the labor-intensive, high-touch processes that typically go into college advising and financial coaching. Where possible, repurposing existing platforms/technologies to test core assumptions is preferred.

Items to consider:

- Do we know whether the tool would be better deployed in a mobile-ready, browser-based implementation (i.e., agnostic to hardware device used; accessible on a desktop or laptop, etc.) or a native smartphone implementation? (One good indicator might be the percentage of FAFSAs that are completed on smartphones.)

- Are there existing platforms that could be used in a pilot to test some of the hypotheses we have? (e.g., text messaging platforms.)

Design Objectives

The design of the tool should:

- **Provide students access to reliable, vetted information.** Information on accessing financial aid and making college decisions is unstructured, disaggregated and often unreliable. The problem is not too little information — there's too much, and it's too difficult to sift through the noise.
- **Reach students at the optimal time in the decision-making process.** Students need just-in-time information — not too early, not too late. They need it at their fingertips as they're making their decisions.
- **Acknowledge, accommodate and analyze student financial history/preferences.** Key data points include eligibility for free or reduced cost lunch, income, savings amount, debt aversion, FAFSA.
- **Acknowledge, accommodate and analyze student academic history/preferences.**
- Key data points include grades, test scores, desired major, desired career.
- **Call out and incorporate key calendar milestones in the decision-making process, including FAFSA submission dates.**
- **Ensure the security and privacy of its users' information.**

More broadly, the tool should:

- Be informed by market insights from financial advisors and coaches currently working with students on financial aid and financial decision making.
- Integrate with existing forms and systems (i.e., FAFSA, bank accounts) in order to pull in and automate as much of the analysis as possible and reduce data re-entry.

Overall Style/Look

This generation of students consists of digital natives. They expect a high level of quality and performance in their user experience and will be attuned to differences and gaps. If built as a native smartphone application, the solution should conform to native patterns and interface guidelines of Android and iOS. If built as a Web app, the solution should be optimized for mobile viewing/built using current responsive design best practices.

If the primary users of this technology come from a low-income background, considerations should be made around maintaining a low memory footprint. Students often have very little free space on their phones, and this real estate can be highly contested. A lower footprint required to install and maintain the app on a smartphone can increase the likelihood that students will continue to keep the app and use it over time.

Inspiration Points:

- "A Siri for higher ed decision making."
- "A Fitbit for higher ed decision making."

Appendix: Expert Insights

Examples of existing online websites, tools, and programs that help young people make smarter financial decisions around higher education:

CashCourse

Age Range: College; **Supports:** Students;

Website: http://info.cashcourse.org/ **Description:** CashCourse was created by the National Endowment for Financial Education (NEFE). The program helps students build money management skills and survive in a tough economy using online financial education materials about real-life behaviors. There is no game component.

Financial Avenue (offered through Inceptia)

Age Range: High school, college; **Supports:** Students, teachers;

Website: https://fa.financialavenue.org/

Description: Inceptia, a division of the National Higher Education Loan Program, offers its Financial Avenue to teach young people about smart money management and a variety of topics that affect their personal finances such as college planning and careers. It offers 30- minute courses on budgeting, credit cards, credit history and paying for college, as well as mini-modules on topics like understanding a paycheck and borrowing money (all based on real-life behavior). There are no games.

MoneyU

Age Range: High school, college; **Supports:** Students;

Website: https://moneyu.com/ **Description:** MoneyU is a computer-based program that incorporates audio, video, animation, interactive tools, supplemental online articles and activities (though no true games) on personal finance and investing based on real-life scenarios and behaviors. MoneyU is available for a fee of $20/student or it can be purchased on an individual basis for $60. MoneyU was created by an eLearning development company and a successful entrepreneur, so the company has no ties to the financial industry.

Save Up

Age Range: High school, adults; **Supports:** Students, adults;

Website: https://www.saveup.com/

Description: The app allows users to keep track of their finances in one place, track their progress on financial goals and play games for free prizes. After downloading the app, users register their financial accounts and credit cards on the app. Deposits in any checking or savings account and payments on credit cards earn users credits that can be used to play games for prizes.

Financial Aid Toolkit

Age Range: High school, college, adults; **Supports:** Students, adults; **Website:** http://www.financialaidtoolkit.ed.gov/tk/

Description: The Financial Aid Toolkit provides federal student aid information and outreach tools for counselors, college access professionals, nonprofit mentors and others.

Consumer Financial Protection Bureau

Age Range: High school, college, adults; **Supports:** Students, adults; **Website:** http://www.consumerfinance.gov/paying-for-college/

Description: When it comes to choosing a college, the Consumer Financial Protection Bureau's Paying for College tool can help students and families make informed financial decisions about paying for college, understand loan options, compare financial aid offers and learn about student banking.

Adventures in Education

Age Range: High school, college, adults; **Supports:** Students, adults; Website: http://www.aie.org/

Description: Adventures in Education is a public service website developed to help students plan and complete their journey through higher education. By providing free resources to students, parents, counselors, and educators, AIE encourages individuals to discover and pursue educational opportunities.

Unigo

Age Range: High school, college, adults; **Supports:** Students, adults; **Website:** https://www.unigo.com/

Description: This free college planning tool helps students find the perfect college based on their goals, anticipated college major and other personal preferences, as well as the best return on investment.

College Board: Big Future

Age Range: High school, college, adults; **Supports:** Students, adults, educators; Website: https://bigfuture.collegeboard.org/

Description: Big Future is an online resource that helps students with everything from finding and paying for college to exploring careers and making a plan. It is an organization that ultimately connects students to college success and opportunity.

Get Schooled

Age Range: High school, college, adults; **Supports:** Students, adults; **Website:** https://getschooled.com/dashboard

Description: Get Schooled is a national nonprofit founded on the belief that students themselves have the power to improve their future if given the right information and motivation. They leverage the key influences in teens' lives to directly motivate them to stay committed to graduating from high school and going on to college. They have tools and resources that help students with FAFSA, applying to college and also finding money for college.

uAspire

Age Range: High school, college, adults; **Supports:** Students, adults; **Website:** https://www.uaspire.org/

Description: uAspire works to ensure that all young people have the financial information and resources necessary to find an affordable path to — and through — a post-secondary education. Through their work, college-ready students have the support and knowledge they need to overcome financial barriers and succeed in college.

College Abacus

Age Range: High school, college, adults; **Supports:** Students, adults; **Website:** https://collegeabacus.org/

Description: College Abacus is a one-stop, secure search site that allows students to compare the net price of nearly 4,000 colleges. The net price is the cost of school after grants and scholarships are subtracted from the total cost of education. The site provides real-time information and is free to everyone.

College Board: YouCanGo! **Age Range:** High school, college http://youcango.collegeboard.org/

Description: An online resource that provides prospective college students reasons for attending college, student stories integrated with topics such as what may be holding them back, college options and next steps, as well as the opportunity to make a pledge to let people know why they are going.

Alltuition

Age Range: High school, college; **Supports:** Students, adults; **Website:** https://www.alltuition.com/

Description: Alltuition.com makes sure students don't miss out on financial aid. Based on the colleges where they are applying for aid, Alltuition instantly matches students to opportunities and helps them maximize their chances for aid.

Packback

Age Range: College; **Supports:** Students;

Website: http://packbackbooks.com/

Description: Packback rents textbooks instantly on a computer for $5 or less per day. Students can rent the same text all semester, and it credits back any money spent on rentals towards the purchase of the book.

Disclosure: Fees may be associated with some of programs, tools and resources, listed. This non-exhaustive list should not be interpreted as an endorsement by the Council or Council members. Members of the Council may have an affiliation with some of the programs, tools and resources listed.

Appendix C: Report of the "Leveraging Cities and Communities for Financial Capability Leadership" Working Group

The Cities and Communities Working Group (CCWG) focused on developing strategies to directly engage cities and communities as leaders in building the financial capability of youth and young adults.

Local and tribal governments have the trust of the community and the power to directly reach constituents.

Both are necessary to effect real change and ensure more communities, especially low-income, minority and underserved residents, are financially empowered. By leveraging the power of local and tribal governments to integrate financial capability strategies into local programming that serves young Americans, and building on strong community institutions such as our nation's libraries and community colleges, we can greatly increase the financial security of future generations.

The Cities and Communities Working Group first established a set of criteria to guide the development of the recommendations. The CCWG determined that all recommendations of this working group must:

- be directly connected to federal policy/programs in order to drive real change;
- be specifically linked to opportunities that harness the unique ability of local and tribal governments to foster financial capability through service integration;
- be actionable, realistic and based on proven approaches; and
- positively impact large numbers of young people.

Based on these guiding principles, the Cities and Communities Working Group crafted recommendations focused on four core financial capability priorities:

- The integration of financial capability practices into youth training and employment programs.
- The expansion of child savings programs to help families save early and often for post-secondary education.
- The protection of young people from identity theft and credit abuse.
- The use of "place-based" strategies to leverage community hubs.

Recommendations

Integrate Financial Capability Practices into Youth Training and Employment Programs.

These programs — largely supported by the Department of Labor and implemented by local government agencies and nonprofits — often provide young people with their very first job. A first job means a first paycheck and presents a unique opportunity for young people to make a timely and informed choice about how to manage their money. However, a 2015 report from the Cities for Financial Empowerment Fund found that 51 percent[17] of young people enrolled in summer youth employment programs in five major cities did not currently have a checking account to deposit their earnings.

Young people should be given the opportunity to begin their working life within the financial mainstream and receive their wages via direct deposit to a safe and affordable checking account or prepaid card, so they can establish a relationship with a mainstream financial institution and a habit of regular savings. In addition, financial education that is relevant and timely should be fully integrated into all government-funded youth training and employment programs.

The working group specifically recommends:

- The federal financial institution supervisory agencies, through the Financial Literacy and Education Commission (FLEC), should offer additional guidance on the regulatory landscape that impacts access to checking and savings accounts for young people, specifically those between ages 14-18. The guidance should build on the *Guidance to Encourage Financial Institutions' Youth Savings Programs and Address Related Frequently Asked Questions* released in February 2015.
  - The guidance should include recommendations for product features and account opening practices that promote safe and affordable checking, savings and prepaid accounts for young people.
  - The guidance should clarify regulations concerning the opening of noncustodial transactional accounts (checking and prepaid) for youth under age 18.
- The Department of Labor should encourage youth training and employment service providers, including local and tribal governments

and community organizations, to integrate financial capability practices into youth workforce investment opportunities. Recognizing funding may be needed to fully implement these strategies, to the extent possible we recommend the Department include guidance and technical assistance for strategies that:

- Provide direct opportunities for young people to open checking and savings accounts with partner financial institutions.
- Facilitate and encourage electronic wage payment (direct deposit) to a checking account or safe and affordable prepaid card product.
- Integrate high-quality and relevant financial education and set standards that define what is meant by high-quality financial education.
- Ensure financial education topics help youth prepare for and transition to post-secondary education and training, with an emphasis on helping students understand options for post-secondary education, the return on investment of attending higher education versus working full-time after high school, consequences of student debt and how to apply for financial aid.

- The Department of Health and Human Services' (HHS) Office of Community Services should encourage and support youth training and employment programs to provide Individual Development Accounts for post-secondary education and training to their participants via the Assets for Independence program.
- The Department of Labor and FLEC should disseminate best practices for integrating financial capability into youth training and employment programs via organizations such as the United States Conference of Mayors, the National League of Cities, the Cities for Financial Empowerment Coalition, the National Congress of American Indians and the African American Mayors Association.
- All federal government efforts to promote financial capability through expanded resources and programming should explicitly include tribal governments and other Native nonprofits as eligible applicants/ participants. Federal agencies also should expand their current outreach strategies to specifically market these resources to local programs serving young Americans in Indian Country (which may not be in current community channels), such as tribal credit programs, Native community development financial institutions (CDFIs), tribally designated housing entities (TDHEs), Native workforce development agencies and tribal colleges and universities (TCUs).

Increase the opportunity for all students and families to save for expenses associated with post-secondary education, and other purposes essential to future financial independence, by supporting and promoting Child Savings Account (CSA) policies and programs across the United States.

Research shows that families who have savings designated for post-secondary education are more likely to have children who will graduate high school, enroll in college and graduate from college or other post-secondary education, even when the dollar amounts saved are relatively small. Previous studies also suggest that promoting saving for education not only has a positive effect on high school graduation and college enrollment rates for lower-income students, but also improves their families' financial capability and promotes lifelong asset building. However, too many families lack easy and direct access to savings accounts or to programs and incentives that encourage lower-income families to save.

The working group specifically recommends:

- The Department of Treasury should convene a group of experts and practitioners from members of FLEC, financial institutions, financial technology companies, national nonprofits, think tanks, funders, and state, local and tribal CSA programs to examine the current barriers to scaling CSA programs. This group should focus specifically on the regulatory, technical and legal barriers to setting up and administering child savings programs at the local level and work to find solutions to these challenges.
- Treasury should collaborate with FLEC members to consider identifying ways to make 529 accounts more easily accessible for and more widely used by low-income families.
- The HHS Office of Community Services should support and encourage the use of the Assets for Independence program to support youth savings for post-secondary education or training and should expand the allowable use of Assets for Independence funding to accommodate a wider array of CSA program designs.
- The Department of Education should consider the recommendation of the College Board to use a percentage of Pell Grant funds to establish "education accounts" for low-income students starting at age 11. Funds could be used only for post-secondary educational expenses.
- The Department of Education should consider creating a grant program to support local and tribal governments and community organizations to launch CSA programs. These programs could be tied

to federal priorities, such as Promise Neighborhoods or Head Start programs.

Protect young people from harm caused by errors and financial abuses such as identity theft and credit abuse.

According to the Federal Trade Commission's Consumer Sentinel Network Report, 24 percent of identity theft cases reported in 2014 involved victims under the age of 30, and 6 percent of cases involved victims ages 19 and under. Detecting cases of identity theft and credit abuse, and even errors in cases of mistaken identity, in this population can be particularly difficult, as a victim may not be aware of his or her compromised identity until applying for a first job, utility account or loan. Credit abuse may occur at the hands of opportunistic identity thieves, but also at the hands of family members misusing a child's identity, without malice, for the purpose of opening or maintaining family utility accounts. Moreover, credit may be harmed by unintentional, yet preventable, errors that wrongly link a child's credit history to another party's debts. Greater collaboration between the public and private sector is necessary to address the detrimental effects of errors and financial abuses on the financial stability of all youth, particularly our most vulnerable.

For children in foster care, detection and recovery can be especially difficult. In 2011, Congress passed legislation that requires child welfare agencies to annually pull credit reports for all youth ages 16 and older in the foster care system and to assist these youth in resolving any inaccuracies. A recent amendment to the law will expand this requirement to include youth ages 14 and older in foster care, beginning in September 2015. However, many child welfare agencies are struggling to access credit reports and, when they are accessed, to use them appropriately to provide financial education and guidance, and remediate the inaccuracies or errors found on those credit reports.

- The FLEC member agencies should conduct a landscape review on the issue of credit abuse and identity theft of all minors to better understand the scope of this issue and identify actions that would better protect the identity of all young people and facilitate remediation of any errors or abuses that have occurred. Towards this recommendation, members of the Council gathered a diverse group of government and nonprofit experts, including many FLEC members, in May 2015 to initiate a discussion on the topic.

- Regulators should consider convening stakeholders to facilitate a discussion of what protections and remedies currently are in place for vulnerable youth, what more needs to be addressed, and the varying roles of the public and private sectors in closing the gaps. Stakeholders may include leadership from the credit reporting agencies, law enforcement such as Attorneys General and members of the Financial Fraud Enforcement Task Force, creditors including utility and telecommunications companies, and national and grassroots nonprofits. One important discussion could include how credit reporting agencies can share youth credit reports in a simple, centralized way for child welfare agencies and other youth serving organizations, in a format that is easy to understand and use to build the financial capability of the affected young people. We are encouraged by the Consumer Data Industry Association's May 2015 announcement of the National Consumer Assistance Plan to improve consumer interaction with national credit reporting agencies and data accuracy and quality.
- FLEC members and their partners in and outside of government should disseminate learnings to the field and encourage use of existing training and resource materials on this topic. Trainings and materials already have been developed by the CFPB, HHS and other organizations to assist agency professionals and other financial experts working with foster care youth to understand the requirements of the 2011 directive, how to access and interpret credit reports, and what resources are available to redress any credit issues. Credit Builders Alliance, in partnership with Child Focus, Inc., launched a "credit check learning community" to facilitate peer-sharing and peer-learning. HHS' Administration for Children & Families developed and disseminates the *Financial Empowerment Toolkit for Youth and Young Adults in Foster Care*. The Federal Trade Commission offers a variety of tools and publications ranging from tips for preventing identity theft to step-by-step guidance for victims. Two such resources include http://www.IdentityTheft.govand *Safeguarding Your Child's Financial Future*. The Department of Justice Office for Victims of Crime also works on training and technical assistance to help advocates and allied professionals who work with financial fraud and identity theft victims address and remedy the problems stemming from the victimization. These are just a few of the existing training and resource materials and programs that could and should be further

leveraged to better protect, and ultimately empower, youth around credit and identity protection.

- The FLEC should work with the Department of Justice and members of the Federal Interagency Reentry Council to promote youth financial education and consumer protections for additional vulnerable populations, such as justice-involved youth, with the goal of assisting them in successfully transitioning back into the community.

Identify opportunities for financial education best practices that can be offered at community hubs, such as libraries and community colleges, and develop the tools and resources necessary to disseminate new approaches and practices.

One natural, and often central, gathering place in communities nationwide is the local library. Local, tribal, state and community college libraries have an important role to play in addressing the growing need and demand for unbiased financial capability content and programs.

Community colleges also provide a unique opportunity to support lower-income students with financial education and counseling services to make sure more young people do not drop out of post-secondary education due to financial insecurity. For many Americans, community colleges represent an important chance for upward mobility. But day-to-day policies and operations at community colleges often fail to address one of the key barriers to academic achievement — poverty. Strategies designed to increase financial capability of Americans who are focused on upward mobility are a natural fit to be incorporated into community college operations. Integrating such strategies is consistent with and connected to the many community college statements of mission related to life transformation, upward mobility, preparation for full civic engagement and participation in and contribution to society at large.

- The Institute of Museum and Library Services (IMLS) should encourage all libraries across the United States to implement financial capability programming in a way that is adapted to meet the needs of their community. This may include drawing their attention to guidance materials such as the American Library Association Reference and User Services Association's *Financial Literacy Education in Libraries: Guidelines and Best Practices for Service.*
- The Department of Education should leverage the existing investment in public community colleges to integrate financial counseling, debt management, access to public benefits, budgeting and financial

coaching as a core service offered by community colleges. Libraries are encouraged to consider the resources developed by the Consumer Financial Protection Bureau (CFPB), starting with the Partnership Guidebook, which provides information on how to think through the process of building and documenting collaborations.

- The Department of Education should leverage the existing investment in public community colleges and White House Initiative Higher Education Institutions to integrate financial counseling, debt management, access to public benefits, budgeting and financial coaching as a core service offered by community colleges.
  - The Department of Education should convene partners to develop a strategy that would expand proven financial capability programs such as the Annie E. Casey "Working Families Success Network" and provide bundled financial services to community college students.
  - The Department of Education should draw attention to the best practices report prepared by The Institute for College Access and Success (TICAS) detailing how colleges can help students and families make informed private loan decisions.
- Cities and communities should consider expanding or launching pro bono partnerships with professional financial advisors, such as Certified Financial Planner professionals, to better provide young people and their families the ability to seek financial advice from competent and ethical financial planners who can help them to achieve financial security, starting with budgeting, debt management and saving. The CFP Board of Standards and the Financial Planning Association have longstanding successful experience organizing pro bono initiatives in collaboration with local governments, community organizations and schools, to leverage a network of professionals nationwide.

Summary of Background Research

In order to determine the correct set of recommendations to bring to the Council, the CCWG engaged in the following activities:

- Members and staff of the CCWG met in Los Angeles in July 2014 for a full day of discussions with the Cities for Financial Empowerment

Coalition. CCWG members met with Coalition members and field leaders to discuss a variety of relevant topics and obtain input on priorities and recommendations. Members and staff also attended an event hosted by Los Angeles Mayor Eric Garcetti at which CCWG Chair José Cisneros spoke publicly about the work of the Council. As a result, the Cities for Financial Empowerment (CFE) Policy Committee submitted a letter to the working group outlining the CFE Coalition's ideas for PACFCYA priorities.

- The work of the President's Council on Financial Capability for Young Americans was discussed at the National Congress of American Indians Annual Convention and Marketplace in October 2014. CCWG members heard feedback and recommendations from conference attendees and the FINRA Foundation presented audience-specific findings extracted from the 2012 National Financial Capability Study.
- CCWG members held meetings with several federal agencies to discuss our ideas and receive feedback. This included meetings with the Department of Treasury, the Department of Labor Employment and Training Administration, the Consumer Financial Protection Bureau, the Department of Education and the Department of Health and Human Services.
- CCWG members met with Corporation for Enterprise Development (CFED) to discuss policy ideas to support Child Savings Accounts.
- CCWG members and staff from the Department of Treasury met with a multidisciplinary group of stakeholders to discuss issues of credit and identity protection for young adults. This includes representatives from the Children's Bureau of the Department of Health and Human Services, Federal Trade Commission, Office of the Comptroller of the Currency, Securities and Exchange Commission, Federal Deposit Insurance Corporation, Consumer Financial Protection Bureau, Department of Justice, Credit Builders Alliance, National Crime Prevention Council and National Center for Victims of Crime.
- CCWG members met at the HOPE Global Forum 2015 in Atlanta, Ga., January 15- 17, 2015.
- CCWG member hosted the Detroit, Mich., PACFCYA Forum with City of Detroit; Mayor Duggan to discuss implementation of successful financial capability opportunities for youth.

APPENDIX D: REPORT OF THE "ENCOURAGING INNOVATION AND TECHNOLOGY TO PROMOTE FINANCIAL CAPABILITY PRODUCTS AND TOOLS FOR YOUNG PEOPLE" WORKING GROUP

Working Group Overview

The Innovation and Technology Working Group (ITWG) focused on developing frameworks for responsible innovation in support of financial, educational and other transformational technologies that expand financial access and capability for young Americans, especially in underserved communities.

Recommendations

- Recognizing that improving the financial capability of K-12 teachers is likely to enhance the proficiency of students in the language of finance, the Council proposes a demonstration to develop a technology-based teacher training tool. The tool shall seek to provide incentives for teachers to build their own financial capability and their ability to integrate financial topics into the classroom.
- Expanding access to high quality transaction accounts requires public policies that promote private sector innovation. The Innovation and Technology Working Group calls upon the President to:
    - Expand financial access by encouraging cities and communities to disburse wages electronically via modern, low-cost financial instruments (e.g., electronic demand deposit or prepaid card accounts), thereby facilitating the inclusion of financially underserved youth and other underbanked employees.
    - Promote greater awareness and adoption of real-time electronic payments solutions that meet the needs of young Americans with modern functionalities and tools to help these consumers better manage, move and control their spending.
- Since high quality products exist in the marketplace today, the focus should be on finding innovative ways for cities and communities to partner with responsible financial institutions, technology companies and nonprofit organizations to deliver transaction accounts to young Americans. The Innovation and Technology Working Group therefore calls upon the President to encourage private sector partnership with

state and local governments to design sustainable and inclusive solutions. These solutions should leverage identified best practices including:

- Tailoring financial products and education tools to meet the needs of young people;
- Selecting financial products by weighing the costs, functionalities and risks of various options; and,
- Integrating partnerships with businesses, nonprofits, government agencies, financial institutions and young people.

Innovation and Technology to Support K-12 Educators

Technology can help make the nation's 3.7 million classroom teachers more comfortable with teaching financial capability. Doing so not only will benefit the country's nearly 55 million students, enhance the U.S. economy and make us more globally competitive, it will help our teachers learn the concepts and use them to manage their personal lives. Training our teachers to be financially capable is an investment in our nation's economic prosperity. Unfortunately, many teachers feel ill-equipped to teach financial capability and integrate it into core subjects, like social studies and English, because they are not familiar with financial concepts. Evidence shows that, while over 85 percent of teachers believe personal finance concepts are worth teaching, less than 20 percent actually are comfortable teaching them. We must do more to empower teachers to be financially capable to prepare our students for the real world.

There are a number of financial literacy curricula that provide professional development opportunities, but they may not be reaching all of the teachers that could benefit. Additionally, they may not be focused on integrating financial concepts into other classes. To address this concern, the Council recommends a demonstration project that would use technology to build a tool that engages teachers and provides incentives to build their own financial knowledge, and better prepare them to integrate financial topics into their classrooms,

Innovation and Technology Support for Current and Prospective University Students

Background

The Innovation and Technology Working Group is working with the Post-Secondary Education Working Group to develop an online decision-making tool that combines data analytics and peer mentoring to help students make better financial decisions about their post-secondary education.

Already embedded in students' lives, technology can play an important role in helping students and their families tackle the challenge of planning and saving for a college degree, understanding financing options, and making good choices about post-secondary education. Research shows that attaining a post-secondary degree is an important road to greater lifetime income and economic stability. While the return to additional education generally is strong, many are not obtaining those returns, particularly among low- and moderate-income students. Helping students find programs and degrees that put them on track to meet their goals will result in increased value of the investment in education or training. The benefit of these better choices accrues to students, their families and communities, the institutions, and ultimately, to our whole economy. To face this challenge, leaders from a variety of sectors — higher education, business, government, technology, philanthropy and nonprofit — are creating better pathways to enable more students to explore the public investment of a postsecondary degree, effectively build savings for post-secondary education, make sound choices about their education and effectively manage debt, while building financial independence and autonomy.

The ITWG worked with Post-Secondary Education Working Group to develop a blueprint for pilots that will use the power of technology and one-on-one attention to help students and families make better decisions about post-secondary education and how to pay for it. While pilots may vary, the groups expect that they will consider such topics as:

- Identifying affordable college options that meet/reflect an appropriate financial, social and academic fit;
- Getting the best aid package possible; and
- Evaluating offers based on ROI of the school (and what the student wants to study there), as well as the debt/financial aid package that the student will receive.
- In developing a blueprint, the group will seek to understand the answers to such critical questions as:
    - What technology are students already leveraging that financial educators, college guidance counselors, parents and students can tap into? Rather than guiding students to new technology, can we identify pre-existing technology (apps, websites, tools, etc.) that students already are using and infuse them with resources and healthy "nudges"?

- Given that parents and students often use technology differently, is there a way in which they can use the same product/platform to make shared decisions?
- Behavioral economics suggests that the most effective interventions happen at the moment of decision. What are the crucial moments of decision for college-bound youth, and how can we reach students at these moments?
- Is it enough to leverage technology to gather and provide resources, or does the most effective technology also provide "nudges" to incite behavior change? What might these nudges be?
- What short-term incentives can we provide to encourage students to use technological tools for financial empowerment in cases where financial rewards often are many years down the road? Can we provide short-term gratification for long-term rewards?
- Can technology help bring abstract and large-scale challenges, such as the challenge of saving $50,000 for college, to a digestible, day-to-day level? What tools can we provide to help students make small, daily decisions that will impact their long-term goals?
- How crucial is the mobile component of technology? Given that many low-income households use mobile phones as their sole connection to the Internet, must our solutions be mobile-friendly in order to serve those who need it most?
- What are the most effective solutions currently on the market, and what are their weaknesses? How can we improve upon these pre-existing solutions?
- Is it enough to educate students on how to pay college tuition alone, or is there a need to provide comprehensive personal finance skills as well? How important is mastering day-to-day personal finance as one saves for higher education, and how can technology help us achieve both goals?
- Why have companies been slow to create financial products for the college market? What barriers do they face?

Innovation and Technology to Support Cities and Communities

Background

Cities and communities, through innovative partnerships such as the Cities for Financial Empowerment Fund *Summer Jobs Connect* program, successfully have linked work opportunities to financial education. The Innovation and Technology Working Group supports the Cities and Communities Working Group to further leverage youth employment for financial capability.

According to the FDIC, 24 million U.S. households — an estimated 68 million people — were underbanked in 2013. Young Americans constitute a significant percentage of this underserved population. When youth are underbanked, they tend to rely upon alternative financial services such as nonbank check cashing.

High-quality demand deposit and prepaid accounts are an effective way to leverage municipal summer jobs programs for youth financial inclusion. These high-quality transaction accounts can help underbanked youth build assets while reducing reliance upon alternative financial services. The 2013 National Survey of Unbanked and Underbanked Households found that, relative to other unbanked households, unbanked prepaid card users may be particularly receptive to entering or rejoining the banking system.

The Consumer Financial Protection Bureau (CFPB) and the Financial Literacy and Education Commission (FLEC) convened a roundtable to explore opportunities for communities to add financial knowledge, skills and access to financial products to youth employment programs. In a report about the convening, the CFPB found that many cities and communities lack capacity to effectively train youth employees in practical money skills. CFPB also found that many financial institutions have been hesitant to open accounts for youth because of the temporary nature of some employment programs, while others are concerned about account ownership for consumers under age 18.

A significant percentage of young people employed by municipal governments are reliant upon nonbank alternative financial services, causing a fall in take-home earnings. Enrolling unbanked youth in traditional demand deposit accounts can be challenging because youth employment programs tend to be short-term and small-scale, creating administrative challenges. Moreover, unbanked youth are more likely to have limited or impaired credit.

Innovative financial services such as workplace and college account programs can help youth establish banking relationships and build financial capability. In cases where impaired credit puts traditional bank accounts out of reach, high-quality prepaid accounts enable access to financial services.

APPENDIX E: FINANCIAL CAPABILITY BEST PRACTICES AND RESOURCES

Report from the Working Group on Financial Education for Children

Whether building a new financial education program or choosing among options, educators can use the accumulated knowledge and experience of the field to help incorporate best practices for greater effectiveness. Some may not be aware that some of the key criteria for effective programs is readily known and available. Here the Council shares best practices in programming and evaluation developed in the field to date.

Best Practices in Programming

The effect of financial education programs depends on numerous aspects of instruction, curricula and rigor. As a guide for educators on how to identify and implement successful financial education, the National Endowment for Financial Education has outlined five key factors that all programs should utilize to maximize the effect of outcomes (http://www.nefe.org/who-we-help/educators/five-key-factors-for-effective-financialeducation.aspx).

The 5 Key Factors for Effective Financial Education

- Well-trained educator to facilitate learning;
- Vetted/evaluated program materials;
- Timely instruction;
- Relevant subject matter; and
- Evidence of impact.

Disclosure: The 5 Key Factors for Effective Financial Education may not apply to new or promising programs, tools and resources whose materials have not been vetted or evaluated yet.

The Jump$tart Coalition for Financial Literacy's National Standards in K-12 Personal Finance Education, http://www.jumpstartcoalition.org/national-standards.html, delineate the personal finance knowledge and ability that young people should acquire to emerge as independent adult consumers, fully prepared to make wise financial decisions.

The Council for Economic Education's K-12 Standards, http://www.councilforeconed.org/resource/common-core-state-standards/, lists the Common Core State Standards (CCSS) and identifies CEE resources in alignment with the standards.

Best Practices in Evaluation

To implement a systematic evaluation of the effectiveness of Pre K-12 financial education, the assessments, which the educators may create themselves, should be designed to measure multiple types of information, including: knowledge of personal finance topics; financial management behavior; and confidence in and the aspiration to manage finances. Assessments should cover material that is content and age appropriate, be taught by a well-trained teacher, link directly to the subject matter covered in the class and reflect the local nuance of the class needs.

Knowledge *— Assessment questions that seek to measure the knowledge of personal finance topics should:*

- Cover topics that represent the core financial knowledge subjects of earning, spending, saving, borrowing and risk management;
- Be explicitly linked to the state's financial literacy standards and/or other national financial literacy standards; and
- Link to themes that are timely and relevant for the specific student population.

Behavior *— Assessment questions that seek to measure the application of what the students learn should*:

- Determine if students have opportunities to utilize financial skills outside the classroom in a safe setting;
- Gain insight on how students plan and use financial concepts;
- Assess students financial behavior and participation in the economy; and
- Ascertain the level of accurate application of knowledge outside the classroom.

Confidence — Assessment questions that seek to measure the confidence students have in their ability to use financial concepts should:

- Determine if students have access to individuals, organizations, etc., that they feel they can go to when and if they have personal financial questions; and
- Ascertain whether or not students can make the connection between financial knowledge concepts to their everyday life.

Aspiration — Assessment questions that seek to measure the economic energy and aspirations of students should:

- Determine if students have the desire to be financially self-sufficient;
- Assess if students have the aspiration to participate in the economy;
- Ascertain whether or not students have high levels of economic energy (a combination of aspiration, confidence, skills and mentors); and
- Evaluate if the students have a sense of financial well-being.

Note: These best practices cover all financial education programs, not just those for K-12.

Evaluation Resources

NEFE's Financial Education Evaluation Toolkit, http://toolkit.nefe.org/, is designed to help financial educators understand evaluation concepts and efficiently apply them to their educational programs so they can document the impact their programs have on students.

The Gallup-Hope Index, http://www.operationhope.org/Gallup-HOPE-Index, measures youth attitudes about entrepreneurship and financial literacy to gain insight into how they envision their economic future, including confidence and aspirations, and to understand their level of participation in our nation's economy.

Rigorous evaluation of financial capability strategies: Why, when and how

(http://files.consumerfinance.gov/f/201401 cfpb report rigorous-evaluation-financial-capability.pdf) from the Consumer Financial Protection Bureau defines evaluation practices such as randomized controlled trials, and provides information on effective design, implementation, data collection and analysis in evaluations.

The Programme for International Student Assessment (PISA), http://www.oecd.org/pisa/pisaproducts/PISA-2015-Technical-Standards.pdf, publishes its technical specifications for data collection necessary to preserve the quality of its international dataset and allow for valid cross-national inferences to be made.

APPENDIX F: RESOURCES AND TOOLS

Report from the Working Groups on Financial Education for Children and Post-Secondary Education

There is no one-size-fits-all financial capability program. Different programs exist, depending upon age, knowledge, content, context and the provider. Using the *5 Key Factors for Effective Financial Capability Programs* and information gathered from public comment, the Pre K-12 and Post-Secondary working groups selected the following list of proven and promising financial capability programs for educators who provide services in school; for community organizations; public private partnerships; and technology-based programs.

Disclosure: Fees may be associated with some of programs, tools and resources listed. Although the majority were vetted by the Council using the 5 Key Factors for Effective Financial Education, it is a non-exhaustive list that should not be interpreted as an endorsement by the Council members. Members of the Council may have an affiliation with some of the programs, tools and resources listed.

Programs for School Curricula (Pre K – 12)

- Financial Fitness for Life® (FFFL), Council for Economic Education (http:/fffl.ncee.net) is a comprehensive personal finance curriculum that teaches students how to make thoughtful, well-informed decisions about important aspects of personal finance, such as earning income, spending, saving, borrowing, investing and managing money. (Grades K-12)
- High School Financial Planning Program (HSFPP), National Endowment for Financial Education (NEFE) (www.hsfpp.org) is a turnkey financial literacy program specifically focused on basic

personal finance skills that are relevant to the lives of pre-teens, teens and young adults. (Grades 8-12)

- JA Finance Park and JA Financial Literacy, Junior Achievement (https://www.juniorachievement.org/web/ja-usa/ja-programs) helps students build a foundation for making intelligent personal financial decisions through curricula and hands-on simulation experiences. (Multiple programs for Grades K-12)
- Take Charge Today at the University of Arizona (https://takecharge today.arizona.edu/) provides users with a comprehensive curriculum design, including over 75 lesson plans, instructional support and professional development. [Formerly known as Family Economics and Financial Education] (Grades 7-12)
- Entrepreneurship: Owning Your Future, Network for Teaching Entrepreneurship (NFTE) (http://www.nfte.com/) is a classroom-based curriculum with project-based learning lessons and experiential classrooms to help students develop an entrepreneurial mindset. (Middle and high school)
- Vault-Understanding MoneyTM and EverFi- Financial LiteracyTM, EverFi (http://www.everfi.com/financial-education) use new-media learning platforms with video, animations, 3-D gaming, avatars and social networking technologies to bring complex financial concept to life for today's digital generation. (Vault: Grades K-6; EverFi: Grades 9-12)
- Money As You Grow (www.moneyasyougrow.org), developed based on a recommendation of the President's Advisory Council on Financial Capability, offers 20 essential, age-appropriate financial lessons—with corresponding activities.
- Money Math for Teens (http://www.saveandinvest.org/Financial Basics/Teens/)—created by the FINRA Investor Education Foundation, Channel One News and America Saves—is a series of lesson plans and assessments that explore the mathematics behind personal finance concepts such as compound interest, opportunity costs and more, in a way that's practical and relevant to teens.

Framework for K-12 Education

- *Advancing K-12 Financial Education: A Guide for Policymakers, Consumer Financial Protection Bureau,* (http://files.consumer finance.gov/f/201504 cfpb advancing-k-12-financialeducation-a-guide-for-policymakers.pdf) provides a step-by-step guide to developing and/or enhancing K-12 financial education initiatives. The guide includes multiple case studies and accompanying resources to help interested parties lay the groundwork, build the initiative and extend the impact of their financial education efforts.

Enhancements to K-12 Education

- MoneythinkMobile (http://moneythink.org/our-program/moneythink-mobile/), an interactive social platform that extends the learning opportunity beyond the classroom, empowering students to implement healthy financial habits while deepening relationships and enriching in-class conversations between staff mentors and students. The app was designed through IDEO.org with support from the Center for Financial Services Innovation, and has launched nationally to 1,500 students in 30 communities since October 2014, resulting in an estimated $10,000 in student savings and thousands of "savings moments" documented photographically by students. The app also is being licensed to institutions of higher education such as Ohio State University, for broader reach.

Planning for College

- Education Planner, the Pennsylvania Higher Education Assistance Agency, www.EducationPlanner.org contains resources for students, parents and counselors on college search, funding college, careers and college visits.
- Big Future, The College Board, www.BigFuture.CollegeBoard.org has resources for college planning, finding the right institution, applying to and paying for college, and exploring careers.
- Federal Student Aid, U.S. Department of Education, www.StudentLoans.gov offers resources for undergraduate and graduate students, as well as parent borrowers.
- Paying for College, Consumer Financial Protection Bureau (http://www.consumerfinance.gov/paying-for-college/) , offers tools to help students and former students to make smart decisions about financing their college education. Through this tool students can compare college costs and financial aid offers as well as access information and advice on ways to optimize student loan repayment option.

- Edvisors Network, Inc., (https://www.edvisors.com/) provides comprehensive, expert insights on paying for college from leading financial aid authority and Edvisors.com publisher Mark Kantrowitz.
- Saving for College, LLC, (http://www.savingforcollege.com/) gives parents information about 529 savings plans, Coverdell education savings accounts and other savings strategies.

Community-Based Programs

- MY Path (formerly Mission SF Community Financial Center) (http://www.mypathus.org/) provides disadvantaged youth with peer-led financial capability trainings, a savings account at a mainstream financial institution and incentives to set and meet savings goals.
- Project Ready Financial Capability Program, National Urban League (http://iamempowered.com/programs/project-ready) is designed to foster students' knowledge and attitudes towards post-secondary success. The framework brings together research and promising practices on youth development, adolescent literacy, out-of-school time learning and student success with the tradition and legacy of the Urban League movement.
- Gallup-Hope Index, Operation Hope (http://www.operationhope.org/GallupHOPE-Index) is used to measure youth attitudes about entrepreneurship and financial literacy, to gain insight into how they envision their economic future, and to understand their level of participation in our nation's economy.
- Girl Scouts of the USA, Financial Empowerment K-12 Program, (https://www.girlscouts.org/program/gs cookies/pdf/2012 Financial E mpowerment spreads.pdf) provides girls the opportunity to build business savvy and hone financial literacy skills through curriculum, online learning and the Girl Scout Cookie Program. More than one-quarter of Girl Scouts programs have financial education embedded within.
- U.S. Conference of Mayors' Summer Youth Employment Program (http://bedollarwise.org/) urges mayors to create innovative partnerships with their local business and nonprofit communities to ensure that the nation's youth have a meaningful summer job experience.
- Boy Scouts' Personal Management program (http://www.scouting.org/scoutsource/BoyScouts/AdvancementandAwards/Merit Badges/mb-PERM.aspx) provides participants with a merit badge for

making a commitment and establishing a path to meet short- and long-term financial goals.

Public/Private Programs Emphasizing Internships as a Complement to Coursework

- Ariel Nuveen Investment Program, Ariel Academy (Chicago) (https://arielinvestmentsclass.wordpress.com/) demystifies the financial world by providing an opportunity for the students to manage a real $20,000 portfolio.
- Juma Ventures (http://www.jumaventures.org/) combines employment in social enterprises, college preparation and financial asset building to create a safe, supportive community where low-income youth can achieve their dreams of a college education.
- Magnetar Youth Investment Academy (Chicago), Magnetar Capital Foundation (http://www.magnetaracademy.org/) is a hands-on, innovative financial literacy program for high school students that focuses on financial responsibility and decision making, including a mock stock trading day.
- Career Academy, National Academy Foundation (http://naf.org/) fosters partnerships between the business and education communities to provide opportunities to underserved students, focusing on preparing students for postsecondary education while providing them with the skills and experience necessary to attain entry-level jobs.
- Earn Your Future Curriculum, PwC (http://www.pwc.com/us/en/about-us/corporate-responsibility/commitment-to-youth-education/financial-literacy-curriculum.jhtml) provides students and educators with free and easy access to financial literacy education, including easy-to-follow lesson plans accompanied by interactive handouts.

Technology/Innovation

- Thrive 'n' Shine, MindBlown Labs (http://www.mindblownlabs.com/) is a mobile app/game that engages teens and young adults with real-life challenges such as securing a meal and paying for college.
- My Classroom Economy, Vanguard (http://myclassroomeconomy.org/) is a classroom economic system that teaches financial education through simulation and is designed to overlay classroom curriculum that aligns to the Common Core State Standards.

- Financial Football, Visa (http://www.practicalmoneyskills.com/games/trainingcamp/) is a game that teaches financial and money management concepts through football and is promoted through partnership with the NFL.
- The Stock Market Game (http://www.stockmarketgame.org/index.html)is an online simulation of the global capital markets that engages students in grades 4-12 in the world of economics, investing and personal finance.
- Mint (www.mint.com) is a personal financial management tool that links users to more than 20,000 different bank, credit card, loan and investment accounts. Mint makes it easy for consumers to view all of their financial statements in one place and get a better understanding of where their money is going using tools on basic budgeting, money management and goal setting.

Proven and Promising Post-Secondary Partnerships

- To build financial decision-making skills in college and university students, NEFE created CashCourse (http://cashcourse.org), an online financial literacy program currently used at about 900 schools in the U.S. In 2014, NEFE began a partnership with the California Community Colleges Chancellor's Office (CCCCO) to provide CashCourse to more than 2 million students in the system's 113 campuses. This long-term financial literacy initiative provides valuable resources to students, and lays a framework for critically evaluating the impact of a system-wide approach to financial literacy.
- The Evelyn K. Davis Center for Working Families (http://www.evelynkdaviscenter.org/) is a partnership between the Community Foundation of Greater Des Moines, United Way of Central Iowa and Des Moines Area Community College (DMACC), where it is located. The Center helps families and individuals improve their financial position and connects them with their work and career goals through education and employment services, including training and job placement; income and work supports, such as benefits access and income tax preparation; and financial services/asset building, including financial literacy, credit repair, debt reduction plans and more.
- Skyline College, in San Bruno, Calif., partnered with the United Way of the Bay Area to become the first college in California to host a SparkPoint Center (http://www.skylinecollege.edu/sparkpoint/), a

one-stop financial education and financial coaching service center where clients receive bundled services and resources. The Center provides resources such as workforce and education support, financial coaching, and benefits access, such as benefits screening, a food pantry, pathways to affordable housing and tax preparation. Cañada College, in Redwood City, Calif., partnered with the United Way of the Bay Area to become the second college in California to host a SparkPoint Center (http://www.canadacollege.edu/sparkpoint/).

- The Guardian Life Insurance Company of America created the Money Management for Life^{SM} (MMFL) program (https://www.guardianlife.com/aboutguardian/corporate-social-responsibility) to provide financial literacy training at five partner community colleges to date. Guardian offers a for-credit course with scholarships on personal financial management for students. Guardian now is expanding the MMFL program to provide job training through internships and mentoring.
- The University of Notre Dame's Saving for College program informs families on the benefits of saving for college early and regularly through onsite small group parent sessions, classroom student sessions, webinars, and newsletters and article briefs. Its website (savingforcollege.nd.edu) features information and materials on planning and creating a college savings strategy, and resources for educators and community leaders to use in their outreach.
- Port Jobs, a Seattle-based nonprofit action tank, the National Endowment for Financial Education (NEFE), and Wells Fargo created the Financial Survival Kit for Apprentices program (http://portjobs.org/our-programs/financial-tools). Wells Fargo and American Financial Services co-teach Financial Tools classes to apprentices within the airport, trade, logistics, construction and maritime sectors. The classes focus on money management for new apprentices, who are particularly vulnerable to the ebb and flow of industries reliant on the trades. Several additional unions have adopted this program.
- Community-based organizations and community colleges have partnered to implement various programs based on the Working Family Success Network model. The Centers help low-income individuals and families get on a path to financial stability through a one-stop set of three core services: workforce/career; income support; and financial coaching and education. The Centers are integrated in 16 community colleges in 10 states (http://workingfamiliessuccess.

com/networksites/), helping clients with job placement and retention, family income, credit score improvement, and completion rates for college degrees or training programs. Achieving the Dream is leading an expansion initiative for 15 new colleges to implement the Working Families Success Network model (http://achievingthedream.org/resources/initiatives/working-families-successnetwork).

- Some colleges, such as Elgin Community College in Elgin, Ill., provide independently designed comprehensive financial literacy programs that are not based on the WFSN model. ECC (http://elgin.edu/students.aspx?id=11034) is a resource of financial health exercises and personalized assistance, and its program includes FAFSA events, a Financial Literacy 101 online module, financial aid one-on-one loan advising, personalized loan repayment, career development services, information for graduates, budget workshops and individual financial counseling.

APPENDIX G: FEDERAL FINANCIAL CAPABILITY INITIATIVES

It is important to bring attention to the federal government's involvement in financial capability programs, which covers an array of topics and uses various distribution channels to reach people of all ages. Preparing Americans to make informed decisions about basic financial transactions, such as managing debt, maintaining a budget and saving for retirement are essential elements to becoming more financially capable and are readily available through programs provided by the federal government.

The Financial Literacy and Education Commission (FLEC)

FLEC is the major hub for financial capability efforts led by the federal government. It is charged with crafting a national strategy related to financial education and has created the financial education website, www.mymoney.gov. FLEC is coordinated by the Department of the Treasury's Office of Financial Education within the Office of Consumer Policy and consists of the heads of 22 federal agencies that have a vested interest in American's financial capability.

Federal Programs and Resources with Pre K-12 Components

- Parent and Educator Resources from Federal Deposit Insurance Corporation (FDIC) and Consumer Financial Protection Bureau (CFPB) include a dedicated Web destination for parents, (www.consumerfinance.gov/parents), a dedicated Web destination for teachers, (www.fdic.gov/teachers), and a revised Money Smart for Youth program (https://www.fdic.gov/consumers/consumer/money smart/) , which is a comprehensive financial education curriculum designed to help low- and moderate-income individuals outside the financial mainstream enhance their financial skills and create positive banking relationships.
- The Federal Reserve System has numerous resources from the Board of Governors and the Federal Reserve Banks at https://www.federalre s erveeducation.org.
- Youth Financial Education, Consumer Financial Protection Bureau, (http://www.consumerfinance.gov/youth-financial-education/) offers information to help support teachers, administrators and policymakers interested in building youth financial knowledge skills. Also includes information on ordering brochures and publications.
- The Federal Trade Commission provides resources at http://www.consumer.ftc.gov/features/feature-0022-financial-educators and www.consumer.gov on credit and loans, money, scams, and shopping and advertising for consumers.

Disclosure: Additional funding is needed to evaluate the impact of these and other federal financial capability programs. Additionally, efforts should be made to expand the eligible use of the funds used for these and other financial capability programs.

In addition to the resources described above, there are other federal programs and resources on a range of topics available to Americans. The website www.mymoney.gov is a repository of information from the following entities which are members of the Financial Literacy and Education Commission.

Board of Governors of the Federal Reserve System
Consumer Financial Protection Bureau
Commodity Futures Trading Commission

Department of Agriculture
Department of Defense
Department of Education
Department of Health and Human Services
Department of Housing and Urban Development
Department of Labor
Department of the Treasury
Department of Veterans Affairs
Federal Deposit Insurance Corporation
Federal Emergency Management Agency Federal Trade Commission
General Services Administration
National Credit Union Administration
Office of the Comptroller of the Currency
Office of Personnel Management
Securities and Exchange Commission
Small Business Administration
Social Security Administration
White House Domestic Policy Council

In 2014, the U.S. Government Accountability Office [18] reviewed federal financial literacy programs and identified 13 major financial education programs and three housing counseling programs. While this is not a comprehensive list of all federal programs and resources on financial capability and counseling, the list provides a sense of the scope of existing federal resources.

Financial Literacy Agency	Program or activity
Board of Governors of the Federal Reserve System	Division of Consumer and Community Affairs and Office of Public Affairs
Consumer Financial Protection Bureau	Office of Financial Education and other offices
Department of Agriculture	Family and Consumer Economics programs
Department of Defense	Personal Financial Management Program (located within Family Support Centers)
Department of Health and Human Services	National Education and Resource Center on Women and Retirement Planning
Department of Labor	Saving Matters Retirement Savings Education Campaign
Department of the Treasury	Office of Financial Education and Financial Access (now incorporated into the Office of Consumer Policy)

(Continued)

Financial Literacy Agency	Program or activity
Department of Labor	Wi$eUp
Federal Trade Commission	Division of Consumer and Business Education
Office of the Comptroller of the Currency	Consumer education activities
Office of Personnel Management	Retirement Readiness NOW
Securities and Exchange Commission	Office of Investor Education and Advocacy
Housing Counseling and Foreclosure Mitigation	
Department of Housing and Urban Development	Housing Counseling Assistance Program
NeighborWorks America	National Foreclosure Mitigation Counseling Program and Other housing counseling activities

MEMBERS

The Council is composed of the Secretary of the Treasury, the Secretary of Education, the Director of the Consumer Financial Protection Bureau and the non-governmental members listed below.

John W. Rogers, Jr., Chair of Council, Chairman,
CEO and CIO, Ariel Investments

José Cisneros, Vice Chair of Council, Treasurer,
City and County of San Francisco

Ted Beck, President and CEO,
National Endowment for Financial Education

Sherry Salway Black, Senior Advisor,
National Congress of American Indians

John Hope Bryant, Founder, Chairman and CEO, Operation HOPE

Anna Maria Chávez, CEO, Girl Scouts of the USA

Michael L. Corbat, CEO, Citigroup, Inc.

Kerry N. Doi, President and CEO,
Pacific Asian Consortium in Employment

Robert J. Glovsky, Vice Chair and a Principal, The Colony Group

Ted Gonder, Co-Founder and CEO, Moneythink

Richard G. Ketchum, Chairman and CEO,
Financial Industry Regulatory Authority

Beth Kobliner, Personal Finance Journalist and Author

Lillian M. Lowery, Maryland State Superintendent of Schools,
Maryland State
Department of Education
Kilandigalu (Kay) M. Madati, EVP,
Digital Media and Chief Digital Officer, BET Network

Marc H. Morial, President and CEO, National Urban League

Deanna M. Mulligan, President and CEO,
The Guardian Life Insurance Company of America

Carol E. Quillen, President, Davidson College

Amy Rosen, Partner, Public Private Strategy Group

Charles W. Scharf, CEO, Visa Inc.

Brad D. Smith, President and CEO, Intuit

Regina Stanback Stroud, President, Skyline College

Jason W. Young, Co-Founder and CEO, Mindblown Labs

End Notes

[1] 2013 American Community Survey, U.S. Census Bureau.

[2] For example, 8.5 percent of white students scored below proficiency level 2 (out of 5 score-based achievement levels)[2], compared to 37 percent of African American and nearly 27 percent of Hispanic students. Conversely, 14 percent of white students scored at the top level, compared to an overall average of 9.4 percent of students, and a statistically insignificant percentage of minority students who attained that level. http://nces.ed.gov/surveys/pisa/pisa2012/pisa2012highlights12.asp.

[3] 2012 National Financial Capability Study (State-by-State Survey), FINRA Investor Education Foundation. www.usfinancialcapability.org.

[4]Mottola, Gary R. *The Financial Capability of Young Adults—A Generational View*. March 2014. FINRA Investor Education Foundation http://usfinancialcapability.org/downloads/FinancialCapabilityofYoungAdults.pdf.

[5] See above.

[6] According to the 2011-2012 National Postsecondary Student Aid Study, 71 percent of young adults finance post-secondary education with debt (http://nces.ed.gov/pubs2013/2013165.pdf).

[7] Based on 2014 data from *Mobile Millennials: Over 85% of Generation Y Owns Smartphones* http://www.nielsen.com/us/en/insights/news/2014/mobile-millennials-over-85-percent-of-generation-yowns-smartphones.html and *Ring the Bells: More Smartphones in Students' Hands Ahead of Back-to-School Season*http://www.nielsen.com/us/en/insights/news/2013/ring-the-bells-more-smartphones-in-studentshands-ahead-of-back.html.

[8] Friedline, Terri and West, Stacia, *Building Millennials' Financial Health Via Financial Capability*, June 2015, https://static.newamerica.org/attachments/3330-building-millennials-financial-health-via-financial-capability/MillennialsFinancialHealth.5a49a18e2eab40a5afd1925ef695a1e0.pdf.

[9] Hensley, Billy J., *Content-Based Teacher Professional Development Pilot*, National Endowment for Financial Education. http://www.jumpstart.org/assets/files/Teacher%20Alliance/J$TTA%20Pilot%20Research%20Report.pdf

[10] Urban, Carly, Maximilian Schmeiser, J. Michael Collins, and Alexandra Brown, *State Financial Education Mandates: It's All in the Implementation*, FINRA Foundation. January 2015. http://www.finra.org/sites/default/files/investoreducationfoundation.pdf

[11] Wiedrich, Kasey, J. Michael Collins, Laura Rosen, and Ida Rademacher, 2014. *Financial Education and Account Access Among Elementary Students: Findings from the Assessing Financial Capability Outcomes (AFCO) Youth Pilot.*, http://cfed.org/assets/pdfs/AFCO_Youth_Full_Report_Final.pdf

[12] See http://joinbankon.org

[13] Hensley, Billy J. Content-Based Teacher Professional Development Pilot, National Endowment for Financial Education. http://www.jumpstart.org/assets/files/Teacher%20Alliance/J$TTA%20Pilot%20Research%20Report.pdf

[14] "Millennials & College Planning," Junior Achievement USA and PwC. https://www.juniorachievement.org/documents/20009/20652/Millennials+and+College+Planning.pdf

[15] American Library Association: http://www.ala.org/tools/libfactsheets/alalibraryfactsheet01

[16] http://www.treasury.gov/resource-center/financial-education/Pages/Finemp.aspx

[17] The Cities for Financial Empowerment Fund. *Summer Jobs Connect: More Than A Job: Lessons from the First Year of Enhancing Municipal Summer Youth Employment Programs through Financial Empowerment*, February 2015. http://cfefund.org/sites/default/files/More

%20Than%20a%20Job%20Lessons%20from%20the%20First%20Year%20of%20Enhancing%20Municipal%20Summer%20Youth%20Employment%20Programs%20through%20Financial%20Empowerment.pdf

[18] Financial Literacy Overview of Federal Activities, Programs, and Challenges. Statement of Alicia Puente Cackley, Director Financial Markets and Community Investment. Testimony Before the Subcommittee on Financial Institutions and Consumer Credit, House Committee on Financial Services. April 30, 2014. http : / /www.gao .gov/ assets /670/662833.p df.

In: Building the Financial Capability … ISBN: 978-1-63484-333-1
Editor: Anthony Hodges

Chapter 2

GUIDANCE TO ENCOURAGE FINANCIAL INSTITUTIONS' YOUTH SAVINGS PROGRAMS AND ADDRESS RELATED FREQUENTLY ASKED QUESTIONS*

Board of Governors of the Federal Reserve System, Federal Deposit Insurance Corporation, Financial Crimes Enforcement Network, National Credit Union Administration, Office of the Comptroller of the Currency

The Board of Governors of the Federal Reserve System (FRB), the Federal Deposit Insurance Corporation (FDIC), the National Credit Union Administration (NCUA), and the Office of the Comptroller of the Currency (OCC), as members of the Financial Literacy and Education Commission (FLEC), together with the Financial Crimes Enforcement Network (FinCEN) of the U.S. Department of the Treasury, are issuing guidance regarding youth savings programs. The issuance of this document is also supported by the agencies that serve as the FLEC Chair (the U.S. Department of the Treasury) and Vice Chair (the Consumer Financial Protection Bureau).

---

* This is an edited, reformatted and augmented version of a document issued by the Financial Literacy and Education Commission, February 24, 2015.

The purpose of the guidance is to encourage financial institutions[1] to develop and implement programs to expand the financial capability of youth and build opportunities for financial inclusion for more families. The guidance also addresses frequently asked questions that may arise as financial institutions collaborate with schools, local and state governments, non-profits, or corporate entities to facilitate youth savings and financial education programs. Such efforts are consistent with the FLEC's *National Strategy for Financial Literacy* to advance the expansion of financial capability among America's youth and to increase their opportunities to save.[2]

BACKGROUND

Throughout the country, various financial institutions collaborate with elementary, middle, and high school administrators, and, in some cases, with government, non-profit, or private entity partners to administer youth savings and financial education programs. The youth savings programs are often structured as in-school credit union or bank programs that offer students basic savings accounts. They also may include more complex asset-building accounts and school district-wide programs that offer universal savings accounts to large numbers of children or non-school based models administered by state and local governments and non-profit agencies. Research indicates that youth savings programs may be effective in helping improve long-term financial and educational outcomes, such as completing college.

Youth savings programs are generally linked to a diverse array of financial education efforts, including personal financial management, banking operations, or both. They are intended to help students understand the value of saving for the future by opening and managing savings accounts. These savings accounts generally have very low minimum balance requirements and low or no monthly maintenance fees. Material account terms and conditions are also explained in an age-appropriate manner.

Financial institutions and others involved with youth savings programs indicate that there is some uncertainty about several legal and regulatory considerations relating to these programs and that this uncertainty may cause some institutions to be reluctant to develop youth savings initiatives. This guidance provides answers to common questions received regarding youth savings programs. This document does not create new regulatory agency policy or industry expectations.

Banking Activity Questions

1. Are there restrictions on minors opening savings accounts? How old must a person be to open a savings account without a parent or guardian serving as the custodian or co-owner on the account?

No federal law prohibits minors from opening savings accounts. Rather, a deposit account relationship is based on a contract governed by state law. In general, minors are deemed to not have the legal capacity to enter into a contract, including opening an account at a financial institution, meaning that a contract with a minor is potentially "voidable." However, some states specifically allow a minor to open a savings account. For example, the State of Washington permits a minor to enter into a valid and enforceable contract for a deposit account with a financial institution.[3] States also have different legal definitions of "minor."

Whether it is legally permissible for an institution to open an account for a minor without requiring a responsible adult to be the custodian or co-owner is a determination that a financial institution should make in consultation with legal counsel.

2. Can a minor with a custodial account be issued an automated teller machine (ATM) or debit card?

The Uniform Transfers to Minors Act or Uniform Gifts to Minors Act of each state governs custodial accounts for minors. As a general matter for custodial accounts, a custodian manages the funds in the account on behalf of a minor, meaning the minor would not be able to withdraw funds without the custodian's approval. Therefore, a minor with a custodial account should not be provided with an ATM or debit card that permits withdrawals.

3. Do consumer protection laws and regulations apply to accounts held by or for the benefit of minors?

As with other deposit accounts, various federal and state consumer financial protection laws and regulations apply to youth savings accounts. Applicable federal consumer financial protection laws and regulations include, but are not limited to, the Children's Online Privacy Protection Act (Children's Online Privacy Protection Rule),[4] the Electronic Fund Transfer Act (Regulation E),[5] the Expedited Funds Availability Act (Regulation CC),[6] the Truth in Savings Act (Regulation DD),[7] and prohibitions against unfair or deceptive acts or practices.[8]

For example, the Truth in Savings Act (Regulation DD) requires financial institutions to comply with certain requirements when advertising deposit accounts, provide consumer account holders with particular written information about account terms, provide certain fee and other information in periodic statements sent to consumers, and use specific methods to determine the account balance upon which interest is calculated.

4. Can banks and savings associations receive consideration under the Community Reinvestment Act (CRA) for developing and implementing youth savings programs?

Banks and savings associations may receive CRA consideration if they provide youth savings and financial education programs targeted primarily to low- and moderate-income students. The CRA's definition of "community development" includes "community services targeted to low- or moderate-income individuals."[9] To the extent that a financial institution's youth savings program has a primary purpose of community development, the program will receive CRA consideration as a community development service.[10] In addition, the interagency CRA guidance provides examples of community development services that include establishing school savings programs or developing or teaching financial education or literacy curricula for low- or moderate-income individuals.[11] Financial institutions are also reminded that the interagency CRA guidance provides examples illustrating how financial institutions can determine whether community services are provided to low- and moderate-income individuals. One such example is when a community service is provided to students or their families from a school at which the majority of students qualify for free or reduced-price meals under the U.S. Department of Agriculture's National School Lunch Program.[12]

5. Is a financial institution required to file a branch application when it partners with aschool to offer a youth savings program?

Requirements for financial institutions to file a branch application in connection with a youth savings program vary by regulatory agency. Generally, a branch application might not be required if the primary purpose of the youth savings program is financial education designed to teach students the principles of personal financial management, banking operations, and saving for the future, and the program is not designed for the purpose of profit-making. Agency-specific requirements are summarized below, and financial institutions participating in such programs should contact their respective regulators to determine whether such activity requires a branch application.

FDIC-Supervised Institutions

FDIC regulations permit a state nonmember bank to provide banking services (such as opening or maintaining savings accounts) in schools without filing a branch application or obtaining prior approval from the FDIC if:

- Such service or services are provided on school premises, or a facility used by the school;
- Such service or services are provided at the discretion of the school;
- The principal purpose of each program is financial education. For example, the principal purpose of a program would be considered to be financial education if the program is designed to teach students the principles of personal financial management, banking operations, or the benefits of saving for the future, and is not designed for the purpose of profit-making; and
- Each program is conducted in a manner that is consistent with safe and sound banking practices and complies with applicable law.[13]

Applicable state law and the appropriate state supervisory authority determine branch application requirements, if any, for state savings associations.

FRB-Supervised Institutions

The FRB has not issued branch application policies or regulations specifically applicable to youth savings programs. FRB branch application information is available on the FRB's website.[14]

NCUA-Supervised Institutions

Applicable state law and the appropriate state supervisory authority determine branch application requirements, if any, for state-chartered credit unions. The Federal Credit Union Act and NCUA regulations do not establish any branch application requirements for federal credit unions. The Federal Credit Union Act does provide that federal credit unions were organized for, among other things, promoting thrift among members.[15] This provision is the basis for these credit unions' youth savings programs. In addition, since 2009, NCUA's 5300 Call Report has collected information about credit unions' financial literacy programs, including in-school branches promoting youth financial literacy.

OCC-Supervised Institutions

National banks that seek to set up school-based youth savings programs in nonbank branch settings must comply with 12 CFR 7.1021. National banks that have school-based youth savings programs that do not meet the conditions in 12 CFR 7.1021 must submit branch applications to the OCC.

National banks may participate in financial literacy programs, such as school-based youth savings programs, on the premises of, or at a facility used by, a school.[16] A branch application is not required and the school premises or facility would not be considered a branch when:

- The bank does not establish and operate the school premises or facility on which the financial literacy program is conducted.
- Bank employees work at the site only to participate in the program.
- No services are provided to the general public.
- The principal purpose of the financial literacy program is educational. For example, a program is educational if it is designed to teach students the principles of personal economics or the benefits of saving for the future and is not designed for the purpose of profit-making.[17]

Similar rules are applicable to federal savings associations.[18] Generally, a branch application is not required and a federal savings association's school-based financial education program would not be considered a branch of the savings association as long as the program meets the following criteria:

- The program is conducted on school premises and is not open to the general public.
- Association employees would not be on the school's premises once the program is commenced.
- The association does not establish an office that is owned, leased, or operated by the association in connection with the program.
- The services provided on the school's premises are limited.
- Student accounts would not be established until applications and funds are received and accepted at a home or branch office of the association.
- The association would not be liable for any theft, loss, or embezzlement until funds are deposited and accepted at a home or branch office of the association.

Customer Identification Program (CIP) Questions

6. Does the CIP rule prohibit a minor from opening an account?

No. If a minor opens a savings account, the minor is the financial institution's customer. For example, where a financial institution sends its employees to a school so that students may open savings accounts by themselves without the involvement of a parent or guardian as part of a program to promote financial education, the student opening an account is the financial institution's customer.

However, if a parent, guardian, or third party[19] opens an account on behalf of a minor, the financial institution's customer is the parent, guardian, or third party. The CIP rule states that the financial institution's "customer" is the person who opens the account for a person who lacks legal capacity, such as a minor.

See 31 CFR 1020.100(c)(1)(i-ii)[20] and *Interagency Interpretive Guidance on Customer Identification Program Requirements under Section 326 of the USA PATRIOT Act, 2005 FAQs: Final CIP Rule*, Definition of "customer," FAQ #6.[21]

7. What requirements of the CIP rule apply to a financial institution that opens an account on behalf of a customer, including a minor, such as through a youth savings program?

Section 326 of the USA PATRIOT Act requires each financial institution to establish, maintain, and implement a written CIP appropriate for its size and type of business. As withother accounts, if a financial institution opens an account for a minor, the CIP must include risk-based procedures for: (1) verifying the identity of any customer seeking to open an account, to the extent reasonable and practicable; (2) maintaining records of the information used to verify the customer's identity; (3) determining whether the customer appears on any lists of known or suspected terrorists or terrorist organizations issued by any government agency; and (4) providing customers with adequate notice that the financial institution is requesting information to verify their identities.[22]

8. Based on the CIP rule, what information must a financial institution collect from a customer when opening an account, including for a minor?

Under the CIP rule, a financial institution must obtain, at a minimum, the following information from the customer prior to opening an account:[23]

- name;
- date of birth;
- address; and
- identification number.

An address for an individual can be a residential or business street address or, if the individual does not have such an address, an Army Post Office (APO) or Fleet Post Office (FPO) box number or the residential or business street address of next of kin or of another contact individual.[24]

The CIP rule provides that the identification number for a U.S. person shall be a taxpayer identification number. For a non-U.S. person, the identification number shall be one or more of the following: a taxpayer identification number; passport number and country of issuance; alien identification card number; or number and country of issuance of any other unexpired government-issued document evidencing nationality or residence and bearing a photograph or similar safeguard.[25]

9. How can a financial institution verify the identity of a minor in order to satisfy the CIP rule when the minor is the customer?

Since verification procedures are risk-based, institutions may use reasonable documentary or non-documentary methods to verify a minor's identity. The procedures must describe when the financial institution will use documents, non-documentary methods, or a combination of both. The financial institution's CIP must contain procedures for verifying the identity of the minor within a reasonable time after the account is opened.

For a financial institution relying on documents to verify a minor's identity, the CIP must include procedures that set forth the documents that the financial institution will use. For example, the financial institution might verify a minor's identity using a student identification card.

For a financial institution relying on non-documentary methods, the CIP must contain procedures that describe the non-documentary methods that the financial institution will use to verify a minor's identity. These methods may include contacting a customer or independently verifying the minor's identity through the comparison of information provided by the minor with information obtained from a consumer reporting agency, public database, or other source. For example, the financial institution might verify a minor's identity in an in-school program by having a teacher confirm the minor's identity.

See 31 CFR 1020.220(a)(2)(ii)(A)-(B) and *Interagency Interpretive Guidance on Customer Identification Program Requirements under Section 326 of the USA PATRIOT Act, 2005 FAQs: Final CIP Rule*, Definition of "customer," FAQ #6.

Third-Party Deposit Relationships

10. What are the CIP requirements for customer verification for a financial institution when a third-party (such as a school district or other governmental unit, educational institution, non-profit organization, or corporate sponsor) opens a trust, custodial, or other administrative account at a financial institution to maintain and administer assets for multiple minors?

There are circumstances where a party may create a master savings account with sub-accounts for various minors to save for a restricted purpose (such as higher education). For purposes of the CIP rule, generally, the customer is the "person" (individual, corporation, partnership, or trust) who opens a new account for another individual who lacks legal capacity, such as a minor.[26]

In these settings, the "customer" is the trust, regardless of whether the financial institution is the trustee for the trust. A financial institution will not be required to look through trust, escrow, or similar accounts to verify the identities of beneficiaries of the accountholder. Instead, the financial institution will only be required to verify the identity of the named accountholder by obtaining, at a minimum, the accountholder's name, address,[27] and identification number *(see* response to Question 8 above).

Moreover, the CIP rule also provides that, based on the financial institution's risk assessment of a new account opened by a customer that is not an individual, the institution may need to obtain information about individuals with authority or control over such an account, including signatories, in order to verify the customer's identity.

This verification method applies only when the institution cannot verify the customer's true identity using documentary and non-documentary verification methods.[28]

See 31 CFR 1020.220(a)(2)(ii) and *Interagency Interpretive Guidance on Customer Identification Program Requirements under Section 326 of the USA PATRIOT Act, 2005 FAQs: Final CIP Rule*, Definition of "customer," FAQ #9.

In addition, in circumstances involving accounts for minors established by a custodian, financial institutions should be aware of the requirements for the individual deposits to be eligible for deposit insurance coverage by the FDIC[29] or NCUA.[30]

Other Relevant Resources

- Consumer Financial Protection Bureau (CFPB):
  - Help children build money skills—information for parents and caregivers of children pre-kindergarten through young adulthood: http://www.consumerfinance.gov/parents/
  - Pay for college—consumers can get help to make informed financial decisions about how to pay for college: http://www.consumerfinance.gov/paying-for-college/
- FinCEN:

- Interagency Guidance on CIP Requirements 2005 FAQs: Final CIP Rule: http://www.fincen.gov/statutes_regs/guidance/pdf/faqsfinalciprule.pdf
- General FinCEN Regulation Guidance: http://www.fincen.gov/statutes_regs/guidance
- Questions on the CIP rules can also be directed to the FinCEN Resource Center at (800) 767-2825.

- Federal Financial Institutions Examination Council (FFIEC):
  - Interagency Questions and Answers Regarding Community Reinvestment: http://www.ffiec.gov/cra/qnadoc.htm
- FLEC:
  - Mymoney.gov is a resource to identify other financial education resources from more than 20 federal agencies.
  - National Strategy for Financial Literacy (2011), available at http://www.treasury.gov/resource-center/financial-education/Documents/NationalStrategyBook 12310%20(2).pdf.
- FDIC:
  - Youth Financial Education Letter, FIL-80-2010, November 17, 2010: http://www.fdic.gov/news/news/financial/2010/fil10080.html
  - Youth Savings Pilot Program:
  - http://www.fdic.gov/consumers/banking/youthsavingspilot/
  - Teacher Online Resource Center: http://www.fdic.gov/teachers
  - Money Smart Financial Education program: http://www.fdic.gov/moneysmart
- FRB:
  - Financial Literacy Resources: http://www.federalreserveeducation.org/
  - Branch Application Information (12 CFR 208.6): http://www.ecfr.gov/cgi-bin/textidx?c=ecfr&sid=635f26c4af3e2fe4327fd25ef4cb5638&tpl=/ecfrbrowse/Title12/1 2cfr208 main 02.tpl.
- NCUA:
  - Financial Literacy and Resources for credit unions and the consumers they serve: http://www.ncua.gov/Resources/FinancialLiteracy/Pages/default.aspx
  - NCUA Webinar—Financial Literacy: Putting Your Mission Into Action: http://event.on24.com/eventRegistration/EventLobby Serv

let?target=lobby.jsp&ev entid=756999&sessionid =1&key=7908E 7594C56D7425B316B8D50F95301&ev entuserid=103659848

- MyCreditUnion.gov—Credit Unions in Schools: http://www.mycreditunion.gov/Pages/credit-unions-in-schools.aspx
- An Early Investment in Personal Finance Education Pays A Lifetime of Dividends: http://www.ncuareport.org/ ncuareport/ april 2014#pg11

- OCC:
  - "School-Based Bank Savings Programs: Bringing Financial Education to Students," OCC's *Community Development Insights* report: http://www.occ.gov/topics/community-affairs/publications/ insights/insightsschool-based-bank-savings-programs.pdf
  - OCC Interpretive Letter No. 839, November 1998: http:// www.occ.gov/static/interpretations-and-precedents/nov98/int839.pdf
  - OCC Advisory Letter 2001-1, "Financial Literacy" (January 16, 2001): http://www.occ.gov/static/news-issuances/memos-advisory - letters/2001/advisoryletter-2001-1.pdf
  - 12 CFR 7.1021 [66 FR 34791 (July 2001)]: http://www. ecfr.gov/cgi-bin/textidx?SID=70966f64398a9aa52c 0695f8deef7de2&node=12:1.0.1.1.7.1.25.20&rgn= div8]
  - Office of Thrift Supervision Opinion Letter, Proposal to Create a School Partnership Program (November 20, 1992): http://www.occ.gov/topics/community-affairs/resource-directories/ financialliteracy/opinion-letter.pdf
  - Other resources can be found on the OCC's Financial Literacy Resource Directory: http://www.occ.gov/ topics/community-affairs/resource-directories/financialliteracy/index-financial-literacy.html
- Treasury:
  - Financial Education and Account Access Among Elementary Students: Assessing Financial Capability Outcomes Pilot. Both the full report and research brief are available through http://www.treasury.gov/resource-center/financial-education/Pages/default.aspx.

End Notes

[1] This guidance uses the term "financial institution" or "institution" to refer to all federally insured depository institutions.

[2] "Promoting Financial Success in the United States: National Strategy for Financial Literacy 2011," available at http://www.treasury.gov/resource-center/financial-education/Documents/NationalStrategyBook_12310%20(2).pdf.

[3] See Rev. Code of Wash. 30.22.070.

[4] Children's Online Privacy Protection Act of 1998, 15 U.S.C. 6501 et seq.; 16 CFR Part 312 (Children's Online Privacy Protection Rule).

[5] Electronic Fund Transfer Act, 15 U.S.C. 1693 et seq.; 12 CFR Part 1005 (Regulation E).

[6] Expedited Funds Availability Act, 12 U.S.C. 4001 et seq.; 12 CFR Part 229 (Regulation CC).

[7] Truth in Savings Act, 12 U.S.C. 4301 et seq.; 12 CFR Part 1030 (Regulation DD).

[8] Federal Trade Commission Act, Section 5, 15 U.S.C. 45(a).

[9] See 12 CFR 25.12(g)(2), 195.12(g)(2), 228.12(g)(2), 345.12(g)(2).

[10] See Interagency Questions and Answers Regarding Community Reinvestment __.12(h) – 8, 75 Fed. Reg. 11642, 11649-11651 (March 11, 2010), available at http://www.ffiec.gov/cra/pdf/2010-4903.pdf ("interagency CRA guidance"). See also Interagency Questions and Answers Regarding Community Reinvestment, __.12(i) – 3, 78 Fed. Reg. 69671, 69678 (November 20, 2013), available at http://www.gpo.gov/fdsys/pkg/FR-2013-11-20/pdf/2013-27738.pdf.

[11] See Interagency Questions and Answers Regarding Community Reinvestment __.12(i) – 3, 78 Fed. Reg. 69671, 69678.

[12] See Interagency Questions and Answers Regarding Community Reinvestment __.12(g)(2) – 1, 78 Fed. Reg. 69671, 69677-78.

[13] See 12 CFR 303.46 and 73 FR 35337 (June 23, 2008).

[14] See http://www.federalreserve.gov/bankinforeg/topics/applications.htm. See also 12 CFR 208.6.

[15] See 12 U.S.C. 1752(1).

[16] See OCC Interpretive Letter No. 839, November 1998, available at http://www.occ.gov/static/interpretations-andprecedents/nov98/int839.pdf; OCC Advisory Letter 2001-1, "Financial Literacy" (January 16, 2001), available at http://www.occ.gov/static/news-issuances/memos-advisory-letters/2001/advisory-letter-2001-1.pdf; and 12 CFR 7.1021 [66 Fed. Reg. 34791 (July 2001)].

[17] See "School-Based Bank Savings Programs: Bringing Financial Education to Students," OCC Community Developments Insights report (April 2009), available at http://www.occ.gov/topics/communityaffairs/publications/insights/insights-school-based-bank-savings-programs.pdf.

[18] See Office of Thrift Supervision Opinion Letter, Proposal to Create a School Partnership Program (November 20, 1992), available at http://www.occ.gov/topics/community-affairs/resource-directories/financial-literacy/opinionletter.pdf.

[19] See Question 10.

[20] In March 2010, FinCEN transferred its regulations from 31 CFR Part 103 to 31 CFR Chapter X. References to FinCEN regulations in this guidance are cited in their current format, while regulations referenced in the CIP FAQs use the format in existence at the time the FAQs were first published. FinCEN's website has a tool for the purpose of converting the old citation format to the new one, and vice versa.

[21] See http://www.fincen.gov/statutes regs/guidance/pdf/faqsfinalciprule.pdf.

[22] See 31 CFR 1020.220(a).
[23] See 31 CFR 1020.220(a)(2)(i).
[24] See 31 CFR 1020.220(a)(2)(i)(A)(3)(i)-(ii).
[25] See 31 CFR 1020.220(a)(2)(i)(A)(4).
[26] See 31 CFR 1020.100(c)(1).
[27] An address for a person other than an individual is defined as a principal place of business, local office, or other physical location. See 31 CFR 1020.220(a)(2)(i)(A)(3)(iii).
[28] See 31 CFR 1020.220(a)(2)(ii)(C).
[29] 12 CFR 330.5.
[30] 12 CFR 745.

In: Building the Financial Capability … ISBN: 978-1-63484-333-1
Editor: Anthony Hodges

Chapter 3

PROMOTING FINANCIAL SUCCESS IN THE UNITED STATES: NATIONAL STRATEGY FOR FINANCIAL LITERACY 2011*

Financial Literacy and Education Commission

INTRODUCTION

The recent economic crisis has highlighted how essential it is that individuals and families have the information, education, and tools that they need to make good financial decisions in an increasingly complex U.S. and global financial system. Indeed, as we have learned, the financial difficulties of individuals and families can dramatically affect the financial health of local communities and regional markets. The crisis has also illustrated that the financial well-being of individuals and families is fundamental to national financial stability, and that a lack of financial literacy is one barrier that can lower standards of living and limit prosperity.

The Financial Literacy and Education Commission (FLEC) sets forth here a framework—Promoting Financial Success in the United States: National Strategy 2011 —to provide the foundation for an overarching financial literacy strategy. It also establishes concrete goals that the non-profit, government, and private sectors can and should work together to increase financial literacy and improve financial decision making by

* This is an edited, reformatted and augmented version of a document issued in 2011.

individual Americans and their families as they pursue personal financial objectives. In recognition of the many changes needed to move our nation forward in this regard, the focus in this strategic framework is on (1) the need for increased financial literacy and effective financial decision making and (2) the educational efforts required to achieve those worthy objectives.

The framework identifies five action areas—policy, education, practice, research, and coordination. Not every stakeholder will engage in all five, but carrying out the national strategy will require that each find its own balanced blend to ensure effective participation.

Congress established FLEC through passage of the Fair and Accurate Credit Transactions (FACT) Act of 2003. FLEC is comprised of 22 federal entities and is chaired by the Treasury Department. One of FLEC's primary responsibilities is to develop a national strategy to promote financial literacy and education. In 2006, FLEC developed its first national strategy, Taking Ownership of the Future: The National Strategy for Financial Literacy, which reviewed the progress toward financial literacy at that time and proposed calls to action in four areas deemed crucial to the promotion of financial education:[1]

1. building public awareness of available resources;
2. developing tailored, targeted materials and dissemination strategies;
3. tapping into effective partnerships; and
4. supporting research and evaluation of financial education programs.

Development of the National Strategy 2011

In July 2009, the Treasury Department convened a special FLEC meeting to review the Commission's approach to carrying out its purpose and role. As part of that process, FLEC members set up a working group to craft a new national strategy. Over the ensuing months, FLEC's National Strategy Working Group (NSWG) undertook a comprehensive and inclusive process that included reviewing strategic documents from other nations and other agencies as well as reaching out for input to a wide range of stakeholders in the field of financial education. From this process, and building upon the 2006 strategy, the NSWG identified four goals for the National Strategy 2011:

1. increase awareness of and access to effective financial education;
2. determine and integrate core financial competencies;
3. improve financial education infrastructure; and

4. identify, enhance, and share effective practices.

As part of this inclusive process to develop the National Strategy 2011, the Treasury Department, on behalf of FLEC, published a request for comments in the Federal Register on September 3, 2010. There were 69 unique responses to the Federal Register Notice, with 29 percent of responses coming from non-profits, 20 percent from private businesses, 18 percent from trade associations, 15 percent from private citizens, and 12 percent from the public sector—mostly state-level official commenters. Officials from three foreign nations also responded.

Comments showed significant support for the National Strategy 2011's vision, mission, goals, and objectives: 89 percent of the respondents agreed with the vision, 87 percent agreed with the mission, 81 percent agreed with the goals, and 94 percent agreed with the objectives.[2] The NSWG carefully considered all the comments, and made revisions to the National Strategy 2011 to enhance its clarity and usefulness.

Implementation of the National Strategy 2011

The purpose of the National Strategy 2011 is to create an overarching strategic framework that all organizations involved with personal finance education, research, practice, and policy will find useful to help guide their work over the next several years. The aim is for stakeholders across the country—within the federal government and beyond—to develop, implement and evaluate specific objectives that support and advance the elements of the national strategy as we work together to achieve our shared vision of financial well-being for all people in the United States.

By design, the framework for the National Strategy 2011 represents a broad overview. Achieving the strategy's mission requires that each organization, individually and collectively, implement effective tactics. FLEC suggests ways that organizations can implement the strategy. However, this is not the final implementation plan. FLEC will continue to work on recommendations for how FLEC, its members and other organizations can best incorporate the strategy into their activities and initiatives, and will release an implementation plan in 2011.

As a first step in the implementation process, FLEC recommends that all organizations involved with personal-finance education, research, practice, and policy should:

- embrace the strategy mission,
- distribute the strategy widely,
- choose one or more of the goals and build relevant, measurable objectives,
- seek opportunities to coordinate efforts with others, and
- focus on evidence-based outcomes.

At the federal level, FLEC recommends that each of its members use the National Strategy 2011 to inform and complement their own efforts at promoting financial literacy and education.

In addition, FLEC will take the following steps:

- ask each FLEC member to incorporate the mission, vision, and goals of the National Strategy 2011 into their respective programs and activities as appropriate.
- incorporate the National Strategy 2011 goals and related objectives into the work of each FLEC working group so that FLEC can test approaches, provide best practices, and report on results.[3]
- provide leadership in promoting the National Strategy 2011 goals and objectives that are national in scope.
- coordinate with the President's Advisory Council on Financial Capability on the level of progress in achieving the goals and objectives of the National Strategy 2011.
- encourage the implementation of a pilot program of stakeholders to identify customized strategies that address local needs.
- coordinate with the newly formed Consumer Financial Protection Bureau on its efforts to implement the National Strategy 2011.

PROMOTING FINANCIAL SUCCESS IN THE UNITED STATES:NATIONAL STRATEGY FOR FINANCIAL LITERACY 2011

Vision

Sustained financial well-being for all individuals and families in the United States.

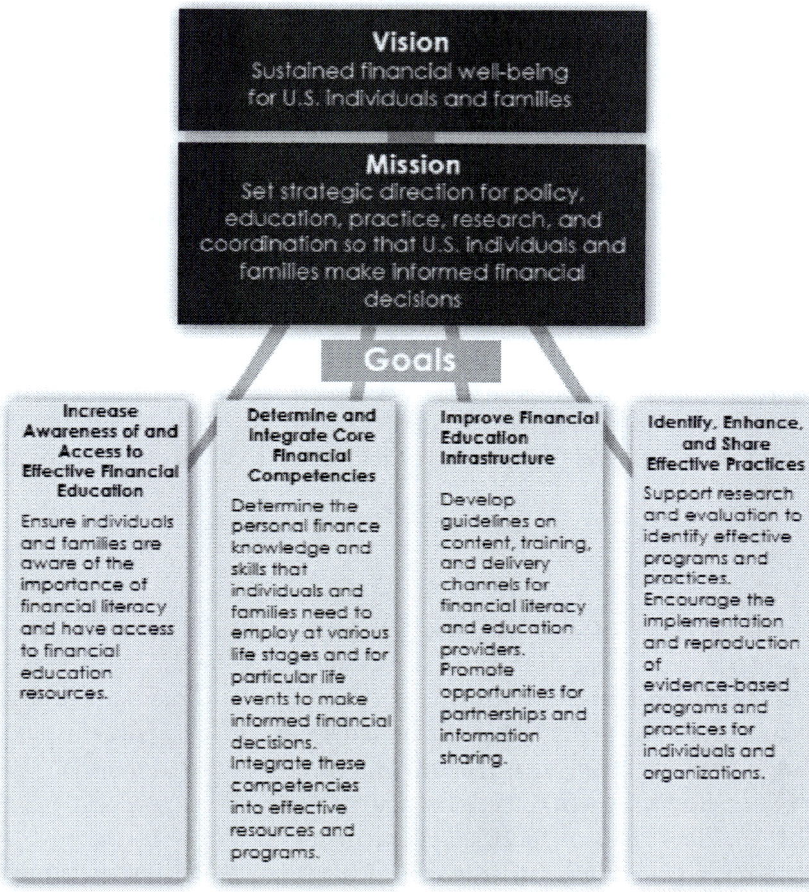

National Strategy 2011 establishes a long-term vision of financial well-being, financial stability, and financial security for the diverse U.S. populace. The National Strategy 2011 seeks to foster a culture in which households take periodic stock of their financial situations, individuals seek information and ask questions before entering into financial transactions, and everyone has the information and tools needed to help manage debt, save to meet their financial goals, and plan for secure financial futures. The subsequent mission, goals, and objectives of the National Strategy 2011 have been formulated to help move our nation toward this aspirational vision.

Mission

Set strategic direction for policy, education, practice, research, and coordination so that U.S. individuals and families make informed financial decisions.

The mission of the National Strategy 2011 outlines the general areas of action that have been identified as critical in moving toward FLEC's vision. These action areas—policy, education, practice, research, and coordination—are influenced by all participants in the field of financial education, from the federal government and national organizations, to state and regional organizations, to communities, and neighborhoods, all of which help ensure that diverse and underserved populations are reached. Not every organization will engage in all five of these action areas, but the National Strategy 2011 relies on each organization to find its own balanced blend of effective work.

Goals

The National Strategy 2011 identifies four goals and related objectives to help move the nation, over the next several years, toward the vision and mission outlined above. Some of these goals seem best suited to the federal government; others might be better achieved by state or local governments, the private sector, or through collaborative efforts. Thus, the recommended goals serve not necessarily as a course of action for the federal government only, but rather for the field of financial education as a whole. Furthermore, the objectives provided for each goal are demonstrative and not exhaustive—organizations are encouraged to develop additional objectives in order to advance the identified goals.

Goal 1: Increase Awareness of and Access to Effective Financial

Education

Although financial education alone does not guarantee financial success, it is nevertheless important that all individuals and families, including those of diverse and underserved populations, are aware of and have access to reliable, clear, timely, relevant and effective financial information and educational resources. Likewise, it is important that individuals and families have access to effective financial education resources disseminated through many different channels, such as schools, employers, and financial education providers. A recent U.S. survey of financial capability[4] found that many individuals both overestimate their financial knowledge and lack an understanding of key financial concepts.[5]

Objectives for Goal 1

- Encourage the dissemination and the development of financial education resources and programs that effectively deliver relevant information to diverse constituencies. Build on traditional practices, community strengths, and research on effective approaches and delivery methods.
- Promote a national media campaign to improve financial literacy, including the use of venues and technologies to reach people where they reside.
- Develop a coordinated support structure for distributing financial literacy and education information, including websites and other resources linking people to educational resources and services that are available on a local and national scope.
- Promote safe, reliable, and easy-to-use consumer resources and tools that can be used during different life stages and when experiencing key life events.
- Promote targeted messages about financial literacy in consumer and employee materials.
- Provide unbiased and understandable financial education resources at financial decision points, such as during the home-buying and college-financing, and as part of the educational strategies shared in schools, colleges, and career and technical centers as well as workplaces.

Goal 2: Determine and Integrate Core Financial Competencies

The development of core financial competencies will provide individuals with the information they need at critical ages and life stages so that they are empowered to make informed decisions. Additionally, core competencies can be integrated into targeted financial education programs and services.

Objectives for Goal 2

- Develop a key set of core financial competencies, and build on them as appropriate.[6]
- Promote the use of transparent, plain-language, and user-friendly forms and information to express core competency topics.

- Encourage financial education providers to align materials with core competencies.

Goal 3: Improve Financial Education Infrastructure

To help ensure that all financial education is consistent, unbiased, and effective, practitioners should follow recommended financial literacy and education guidelines. Additionally, practitioners should foster partnerships and other collaborative opportunities to strengthen the effectiveness of financial education efforts.

Objectives for Goal 3

- Encourage the dissemination and the development of financial education resources and programs that deliver effectively relevant information to diverse constituencies. Build on traditional practices and community strengths.
- Develop guidelines related to research findings, core competencies, curriculum development, delivery methods, and program evaluation that could be used by financial education providers and counselors.
- Establish clear financial literacy training goals and strategies that stakeholders can use to enhance the consistency and quality of program planning, delivery, and evaluation.
- Develop recommendations for professional development courses and incentives for financial education providers, identify best practices for organizational accreditation, and provide other support for financial education practitioners.
- Set up a network of financial education providers and counselors and provide opportunities for information-sharing.
- Create strategies for partnerships, mentors or coaches, and other mechanisms for enhancing the delivery and effectiveness of financial education in schools, colleges, and career and technical centers as well as in the workplace.
- Strengthen connections among those working on financial education, financial access, and asset building strategies to improve effectiveness of each.
- Encourage the incorporation of strategies informed by behavioral economics and the psychology of decision-making.

Goal 4: Identify, Enhance, and Share Effective Practices

Increasing rigorous research and evaluation on financial literacy and education will lead to a better understanding of how to establish effective programs and practices. Implementing and evaluating promising programs and practices in order to learn how to reproduce them effectively also is critical, as is sharing information among researchers and practitioners. Supportive research will also ensure that the field tracks trends, issues, and financial literacy needs in order to remain current.

Objectives for Goal 4

- Encourage research on financial literacy and education strategies that affect consumer behavior to determine the role of financial education vis à vis other strategies for improving financial decision-making.
- Establish a clearinghouse either within or otherwise in connection with existing Federal collections of evidence-based research and evaluation studies, current financial topics and trends of interest to consumers, innovative approaches, and best practices.
- Develop and disseminate tools and strategies to encourage and support program evaluation such as common evaluation metrics to measure key outcomes, behavioral change, and program effectiveness.
- Form a network for sharing research and best practices and updating the evidence base.
- Develop approaches to periodically measure the financial knowledge and decision-making of individuals and families.
- Identify customized programs that effectively address local and other needs, such as those that place emphasis on low- to moderate-income, minority, unbanked,[7] and underserved communities.
- Build upon the research priorities identified at the FLEC National Research Symposium on Financial Literacy and Education in October 2008.[8]

End Notes

[1] The 2006 FLEC strategy can be found online at www.mymoney.gov.

[2] These percentages refer to those respondents who answered the particular question.

[3] In July 2009, FLEC established three staff-level working groups—on Core Competencies, Research and Evaluation, and Communication and Outreach—to support the key strategic areas it had identified. On September 30, 2010, FLEC established an additional staff-level working group on Financial Access.

[4] Financial capability is an individual's capacity, based on knowledge, skills, and access, to manage financial resources effectively. To develop this capacity, individuals must have appropriate access to and understanding of financial products, services, and concepts. Financial capability empowers individuals to make informed choices, avoid pitfalls, know where to go for help, and take other actions to improve their present and long-term financial well-being.

[5] This survey was commissioned in 2009 by the FINRA Investor Education Foundation, in consultation with the U.S. Department of Treasury and the President's Advisory Council on Financial Literacy, to study the financial capability of American adults. A copy of the survey findings can be found on www.finrafoundation.org/capability.

[6] The FLEC's Core Competency Working Group has developed a key set of core competencies. FLEC identified five core concept areas that define what consumers should know to make informed decisions about their personal finances. The "core competency" topics cover earning, spending, saving and investing, borrowing, and protecting against risk. FLEC also identified the knowledge and actions or behaviors that would be associated with each of the core competencies. On August 26, 2010, the Treasury Department—in its capacity as Chairperson of the FLEC—issued a notice and invited public comments on a proposed set of financial education core competencies. The FLEC is considering those public comments in finalizing the core competencies. When those are finalized, FLEC will conduct a public education campaign to promote the core competencies and disseminate core competency resources.

[7] A person who does not have a bank or credit union account.

[8] For a summary of the symposium and the ten recommended priorities, go to www.mymoney.gov.

INDEX

D

H

I

J

K

L

M

N

O

P

R

S

Y